Portrait
of a
Past Life
Skeptic

About the Author

Robert L. Snow (Indianapolis, IN) served for thirty-eight years at the Indianapolis Police Department, retiring in 2007 with the rank of captain. He has written seventeen books and his articles and short stories have appeared in *Playboy*, *Reader's Digest*, *National Enquirer*, *The Writer*, *Police*, and *Saint Detective Magazine*, among others.

To Write the Author

If you wish to contact the author or would like more information about this book, please write to the author in care of Llewellyn Worldwide, and we will forward your request. Llewellyn Worldwide cannot guarantee that every letter written to the author can be answered, but all will be forwarded. Please write to:

Robert L. Snow
℅ Llewellyn Worldwide
2143 Wooddale Drive
Woodbury, MN 55125-2989

Please enclose a self-addressed stamped envelope for reply, or $1.00 to cover costs. If outside the USA, enclose an international postal reply coupon.

Robert L. Snow

Portrait
of a
Past Life
Skeptic

The True Story of a Police
Detective's Reincarnation

Llewellyn Worldwide
Woodbury, Minnesota

FIRST EDITION
First Printing, 2015

Book design by Bob Gaul
Cover images by iStockphoto.com/8043713/©rappensuncle
                iStockphoto.com/21798431/©dlinca
Cover design by Lisa Novak
Editing by Ed Day

Llewellyn Publications is a registered trademark of Llewellyn Worldwide Ltd.

Library of Congress Cataloging-in-Publication Data
Snow, Robert L.
Portrait of a past life skeptic: the true story of a police detective's reincarnation/ Robert L. Snow.—First Edition.
    pages cm
  ISBN 978-0-7387-4656-2
1. Snow, Robert L. 2. Reincarnation—Biography. I. Title.
  BL520.S66A3 2015
  133.901'35092—dc23
  [B]
                        2015027001

Llewellyn Worldwide Ltd. does not participate in, endorse, or have any authority or responsibility concerning private business transactions between our authors and the public.

    All mail addressed to the author is forwarded, but the publisher cannot, unless specifically instructed by the author, give out an address or phone number.

    Any Internet references contained in this work are current at publication time, but the publisher cannot guarantee that a specific location will continue to be maintained. Please refer to the publisher's website for links to authors' websites and other sources.

Llewellyn Publications
A Division of Llewellyn Worldwide Ltd.
2143 Wooddale Drive
Woodbury, MN 55125-2989
www.llewellyn.com

Printed in the United States of America

Contents

In memory of:

— • —

Stella E. Morphew
1932–2010
and
Frances E. Snow
1922–2011

— • —

Love and miss you both.

Introduction

When the first edition of this book came out in 1999, I held the position of captain in the Indianapolis Police Department and had just recently taken over as commander of the Homicide Branch, one of the most sought-after assignments in the police department. Because of my new position, I naturally vacillated about whether or not to publish this book. In the years preceding my assignment to Homicide, I had amassed a considerable amount of stature in the department because of the many magazine articles and books I had written about police procedure. What would publishing a book that claimed I had absolute proof I had lived a past life as a nineteenth-century artist do to my career? I just didn't know.

And even though I gave a detailed account in the book about the two years I had spent investigating the facts of a past-life regression I had undergone and had carefully laid out the over two dozen pieces of evidence that led me to the conclusion I had indeed lived a life before my present one, I still felt uncertain about how it would be received. This was just not something that police captains publicly claim to believe in.

So, because of the controversial nature of this book, I went back and forth for some time about publishing it, some days deciding yes I should, and some days deciding no I shouldn't. This indecision sprang, of course, from my worries that publishing it could have severe and very negative consequences for my career as a police officer, which had just hit a new high with my assignment to Homicide. Even though I had found absolutely convincing proof—more proof than most murder cases—that I had lived a past life, I still worried. What would the top brass and city administrators think of a police captain who published a book about a New Age concept? Would they accept it graciously, or, as I thought more likely, have a much more negative reaction?

I also worried about the effect this book could have on my writing career. Would the publishers of my previous books become concerned about my credibility? Would they think that my venture into New Age concepts had negatively affected my credibility as a serious author of police procedure books? I just didn't know.

I finally decided, however, that I should publish my findings because things had changed for me. I had become a different person than I was before I began investigating what I had experienced during a past-life regression. Before I started the investigation, I had been a stern skeptic who thought that past lives were just a concept dreamed up to explain why bad things happened to good people and vice versa. And while my search may have started out with the intent to prove that past lives didn't exist, the facts I gathered during the two years of investigation brought me to the opposite conclusion: that without a doubt past lives were real. I simply couldn't turn my back on the facts I had found, many of them delivered in a way that gave me chills. My skepticism was gone. And so, to not publish this book after finding fact after fact that supported the existence of a past life—and absolutely no evidence that refuted it—would, I felt, have been dishonest. A police officer gathers the facts in a case, and then lets them decide the outcome.

Also, I decided I needed to publish this book because I found that after my discoveries I had become much more open-minded about concepts I had once scoffed at, and I felt that perhaps my opening up publicly could help others also open up. Along with this, I discovered that my acceptance of the reality of past lives put me in contact with many people who willingly shared stories of their own spiritual journeys. Their stories, however, went beyond past lives and also included out-of-body experiences, ghosts and spirits, and several other concepts I would have earlier just brushed off but was now much more willing to consider.

In the end, I felt I had a story that needed to be told. So I did it, and then held my breath.

As it turned out, the effects of publishing this book were both positive and negative. On the positive side, I have received over the years many letters and emails from readers telling me how much my book affected them and how it helped affirm their own beliefs. Also, in the time since this book's first publication I have come into even more evidence that supports my claim of having lived a past life. Several of my readers took it upon themselves to conduct research into my claims and were able to uncover even more proof that what I saw in my past-life regression were actual scenes from a past life. And for the skeptics, I appeared on national television and took two lie detector tests to show that I hadn't made up any part of what I said in this book.

But while it is undeniable that the publication of the first edition of this book had positive effects for me and many other people, my fears of a negative impact on my police and writing career didn't prove baseless. As I will talk about in the new chapters in this edition, the impact this book has had on me has been life-changing.

And yet, despite its negative effect on my police and writing career, I have never regretted my decision to publish this book. Its message, I feel, is far too important to allow any personal consequences to force me into silence.

CHAPTER ONE

I have recently accomplished something that would make even the most seasoned detective nod with approval. I have uncovered evidence that proves beyond a doubt the existence of a past life. The evidence I uncovered in this two-year investigation is so overwhelming that if it had been a criminal case there would be no plea bargaining. A conviction would be assured.

My claim, of course, is a bold and radical one for a police captain to make. Police work remains one of the most conservative, old-school professions in the world, and as a police captain I'm expected not to embrace such controversial ideas, but rather to be pragmatic, sensible, and down-to-earth. A police captain is expected to be rock solid. Talking about investigating past lives, in the eyes of most police officers, would likely put me in with a group of people most officers roll their eyes at and dismiss out of hand as "certainly different."

Even though I held the rank of captain and served as commander of the Homicide Branch at the time of my investigation, police work had never been my life's desire, but something I simply fell into. I grew up in a middle-class family in the Midwest, where my father worked as a yard conductor for the Pennsylvania Railroad. My mother, like most mothers in the 1950s, stayed home as a housewife. She died of cancer, however, when I was twelve, leaving my father with five children: four boys and a girl, with me being the middle child. My father married a woman several years later who had six children of her own: four boys and two girls. We all lived in the three-bedroom house I had grown up in. While it was certainly crowded, it was never boring.

As I said earlier, although I eventually became a police officer, I had never really wanted to be one. When growing up, I had only one desire for a career: to be a writer. Of course, a child saying this usually gets a pat on the head the same way a child saying he or she wants to be President gets a pat. But my desire never faltered. Soon after graduating from high school in 1965, I joined the Air Force. I had actually gone down to the recruiting station to join the Marines, as several of my brothers before me had. But since I went down at lunchtime, all of the recruiters except for the Air Force recruiter were gone, and he turned out to be an exceedingly convincing speaker.

While in the Air Force I worked as an intelligence analyst during the Vietnam War at Yokota Air Force Base in Japan and at Hickam Air Force Base in Hawaii. When it came time for my discharge, I mustered out at Travis Air Force Base just outside of San Francisco. My life plans hadn't changed: I still wanted to be a writer, so in the late 1960s I settled in San Francisco, figuring it would be a good place to start. However, after being there for several months, my stepmother came down with the same type of cancer that had killed my birth mother. My father called me and asked me to come home for a bit.

After I returned to Indianapolis, my stepmother had surgery, and eventually recovered. During this time, I exhausted my funds and had to look for some way to earn the money I needed in order to return to San Francisco. But after I had worked for a few weeks at dead-end jobs that didn't pay enough to get by on, much less finance a return to the West Coast, my older brother Fred, then an Indianapolis police officer (I also had a younger brother who joined the police department a number of years later), suggested that I apply at the Indianapolis Police Department. The Vietnam War was still going on and the police department was experiencing a severe shortage of recruits. The first six months, Fred told me, would be in school, something that I had always done well at, and the pay more than doubled what I could make at the other jobs I had tried.

So I applied to the Indianapolis Police Department, was accepted, and ended up staying there for thirty-eight years, holding the rank of captain for twenty-two of those years. Police work, and the excitement that comes with it, I quickly found out, can be intoxicating and as addictive as a hard drug.

I also discovered that the work gave me mountains of information I could use in my writing career.

On the social front, like many men returning from military service in the late 1960s, I met a girl, we dated, and then we got married. However, this was cut short when she passed away very unexpectedly in 1978. We had no children, and her death naturally affected me deeply. Since the first edition of this book came out, a number of people have asked me if I experienced any paranormal events after her death, and I tell them no. She simply died, and I eventually had to move on with my life.

Some time after my first wife died, I met my present wife, Melanie. She worked in the public information office at the police department. Since I happened to be good friends with the public information officer, I ran into her often. We started dating and eventually got married just two weeks before she became an Indianapolis police officer. She went on to become a child-abuse detective.

As I mentioned earlier, because of the incompatibility of my discovery of a past life with my role as a police captain, during my investigation I didn't share what I was doing or what I had found with anyone but Melanie. I shared my findings with her because I needed a devil's advocate, and she made a good one. Melanie tried, and tried desperately, to come up with alternate explanations for what I had found, particularly when the facts began building up more and more that what I had discovered was truly a past life. Eventually, out of "logical" explanations, she grudgingly began admitting that what I had found appeared truly remarkable.

When, after two years, I had at last completed my investigation, I discussed with Melanie what she thought I ought to do with the facts I had uncovered, since I felt anxious and uncertain about how others would accept them, but still also convinced that they were so remarkable I ought to share them. Melanie thought about it for several minutes. "I'll tell you," she said finally, "I think you ought to just keep your discoveries to yourself. People will think you're nuts."

I argued a bit with Melanie about this, pointing out that she was just as astounded as I was by my discoveries, and that she could come up with no viable explanation other than the one I had.

Regardless, Melanie just shook her head. "Look," she said, "you're a police captain. You're not supposed to be involved in stuff like this. Believe me, people won't understand."

Since I've always found Melanie to be a very levelheaded woman, I followed her advice, which at the time seemed sound. Soon afterward, however, while talking with another police captain about the murder of an Indianapolis police officer, the captain told me about having an out-of-body experience when coming upon the body of this murdered officer. Astounded by this story, but even more by the captain's apparent total lack of fear in telling it, I suspected that such events might be more prevalent than I had thought, so I began discreetly inquiring around the police department concerning any experiences my colleagues might have had with paranormal events. What I found shocked me.

A large number of police officers related, without apparent embarrassment or reluctance, stories about having paranormal experiences. Two officers told me about witnessing objects moving around on their own in a house neighbors had complained was possessed. The police department brass, I discovered, obviously considered these officers' report credible because, though kept quiet, they sent the police department chaplain out to the house with instructions to see if he could bless or exorcize it. Another officer who claimed to have experienced a paranormal event was another fellow police captain who I consider exceedingly stable and completely reliable. The captain told me about how he had seen himself from high above during a gun battle with a group of holdup men. Unlike these officers, up until the time I began investigating the possibility I had lived a past life, I had never had any paranormal experiences at all. Like many people, I thought they were just something that happened in books and movies, not to real people. Before I began my investigation, my life had been solidly normal, so I felt uncomfortable telling others about my experiences. But listening to these officers talk with no reservations or embarrassment, even though these are not experiences pragmatic, sensible, and down-to-earth people are supposed to have, finally gave me the courage to talk about what I had discovered in my investigation.

Up until the time I began my investigation, I also had never really given any serious consideration to the idea that anyone alive today had lived other lives before this. It wasn't part of my worldview. I had been raised in a strict Methodist family by a mother and stepmother who made it their job to see that their children attended church at least once a week, and many times more than once. In all of the hundreds and hundreds of Sunday School classes and church services I attended, I never once heard anyone speak of past lives. And so, for most of my life I thought the belief in past lives and reincarnation was not really an American belief, but only part of certain Far Eastern philosophies and religions. The only ones in America who believed in reincarnation, I mistakenly thought, were people no one took seriously.

I first became aware that some of the people in America who believe in past lives and reincarnation are educated and seemingly normal individuals through a book I ordered from the Literary Guild Book Club. I have always been a voracious reader, and because of this I belong to several book clubs. This love of reading came from my birth mother, who, along with being devoutly religious, also loved books and reading, and tried to pass along this love to her children. In recalling my childhood, it seems that whenever I went anywhere with my mother, the memories always involve going either to church or to the public library.

The book I ordered, written by a respected American doctor who, according to the book club blurb, had previously investigated near-death experiences, told of the doctor's investigation into reincarnation and past lives. The blurb made the book sound interesting in an exotic sort of way, so I ordered it, mostly out of curiosity, the same way I have ordered books about other belief systems I was curious about. It wasn't that I personally subscribed to any of these theologies or beliefs, or even gave the ideas any credence, it's just that I found them and the reasons people believe in them interesting.

I received the book, titled *Coming Back*, several weeks later, and sat down one evening and read the slim volume in one sitting. I found it to be a well-told account of how the author, Dr. Raymond A. Moody, though initially skeptical of the concept of past lives, allowed a friend to hypnotize him and regress him to nine different lives he had supposedly lived prior to his present one. The theory of hypnotic regression to past lives, I thought as I read the book, seemed relatively simple. A therapist skilled in the art of hypnosis, after putting the subject into a hypnotic trance, simply instructed him or her to recall a previous life. Supposedly, according to the book, many people with psychological issues suffer from these problems because of traumatic events they have experienced during a past life, and whose effects have lingered over into their present life. Mental health therapists, Dr. Moody said, have found that hypnotically regressing a person back to the traumatic event in a past life and then letting the person re-experience the event and talk about it often lessens and sometimes completely relieves the symptoms. So, according to mental health professionals who use past-life regression, whether or not the past lives are genuine doesn't really matter. The patients thinking they are real is all that is needed to resolve the psychological problems.

It occurred to me when I read *Coming Back* that since a person under hypnosis becomes very susceptible to suggestion, this technique would, rather than cause a person to recall a real past life, more likely lead to an imagined past life based on something the person has read or seen in the movies but has since forgotten. And while there is this small group of psychiatrists and psychologists who use past-life regression in their practices and believe that these memories of past lives are real, a large number of mental health therapists don't use past-life regression and likely regard any regressions as simply the product of an active imagination. When I met and talked with a number of mental health professionals who regularly use past-life regression and believe it to be real, I sensed that they felt themselves to be rebels and outsiders.

At the time I read Dr. Moody's book, I already knew a bit about regressive hypnosis because it was just then making its introduction into the criminal justice field—it hadn't been a pleasant introduction. Regressive hypnosis was being used not as any kind of therapy, but rather as a way to assist victims in recalling past criminal acts. A number of people had been hypnotically regressed back to their childhood (in this life), and while there recalled being physically abused or sexually molested, usually by a close family member. Reportedly, these events were so traumatic that the subjects had blocked out any conscious recall of them, and it took hypnosis to bring the memories out.

Unfortunately, whether or not any of these hypnotically induced recollections turned out to be real memories, in several celebrated cases they turned out instead to be only suggestions from the hypnotist. The hypnotist had apparently suggested to the person that childhood abuse had to be the reason for his or her present problems. It was the only thing that could explain them. The hypnotist then kept insisting this until the person "remembered" the abuse.

As a police officer I naturally have always tried to stay up to date on any new developments in evidence recovery, so I read up considerably on these false memories of abuse when several of them became newsworthy. The September 1997 issue of *Scientific American,* for example, contains an article by Professor Elizabeth F. Loftus of the University of Washington in which she details several cases of psychologists and psychiatrists planting false memories of childhood abuse in their patients. One case involved a young woman encouraged while under hypnosis to "remember" being raped by her father, a minister, while being held down by her mother. She also recalled aborting several pregnancies caused by her father, who was eventually forced to resign from his position as a minister when the daughter's accusations became public. A later medical examination, however, showed that the alleged victim was still a virgin.

Because of these types of cases, most police officers look upon regressive hypnosis as extremely suspect. When I read Dr. Moody's book, I couldn't help but remember these cases and wonder if past-life recall didn't also involve suggestions from the hypnotist. Police officers themselves will often lead suspects by suggesting scenarios during an interrogation to see if any of them will cause feelings of remorse or guilt and bring about admissions or even a confession. But unlike memories of abuse planted by mental health professionals during hypnosis, any confession a police officer obtains during an interrogation must then be backed up by physical evidence. It is a long-standing legal precedent that a confession alone is not enough for a conviction.

Interestingly, although throughout *Coming Back* Dr. Moody described his experiences while under hypnosis very colorfully and enthusiastically, at the conclusion of the book he hedged a bit and wouldn't say he felt totally convinced that what he had seen during his regressions were actually lives before his present one. You could detect the doubt in his words. For example, in the chapter titled "Conclusions," he said, "I would like to be able to point to something that was proof-positive of reincarnation. But I can't make such a claim … nobody has provided such proof as of yet." Later, he also said, "But it is precisely because reincarnation is what we would like to believe that we must be extremely wary of any apparent reported observations or data that seem to support this belief … (reincarnation) is such an attractive possibility for so many people that belief in it might give rise to psychologically unhealthy expectations."

And that was just how I felt after reading the book. Certainly interesting, but any past-life regressions a person thought he or she might have had while under hypnosis probably came through suggestions from the hypnotist. Otherwise, why hadn't I heard of someone who had factually documented a past life?

Several months after reading Dr. Moody's book, and largely forgetting about it as I went on to other reading, I attended a party given by the Marion County Family Advocacy Center, where my wife worked as a child-abuse detective. While at the party, I became involved in a conversation with another child-abuse detective, Cathy Graban, who also worked as a practicing psychologist. I wasn't aware that Cathy used hypnotic-regression therapy in her psychological practice. As people do at parties, I tried to make small talk, and, after chatting about the recent movies we'd seen, Cathy and I began talking about recent books we'd read. Since I knew Cathy was a psychologist, I recalled Dr. Moody's book and mentioned that I had read it several months before.

"What'd you think of it?" Cathy asked.

I shrugged. "Oh, it was well-written enough, but I don't know. I think past-life regression is probably just people with a lot of imagination. Probably just people who want to blame their problems on something they can't be held accountable for now. And besides," I added with a knowing smile, "if it was true, then how come no one's ever proved they've lived a past life?"

Considering that Cathy regularly used hypnotic regression in her practice, my attitude undoubtedly came across as a bit overbearing, but Cathy remained very gracious as she listened to me. When I finished, she let a few seconds lapse and then politely challenged me to test my beliefs. She wrote on a card the name of a colleague who also used hypnotic regression and, though I don't know what her intention was at the time, I felt that night that she had basically dared me to find out for myself if it was as phony as I thought it was. I'm not sure why I agreed to take the dare, since at that time I didn't believe in hypnotic regression. Maybe it was because it was near the end of the party and I had drunk too much, but most likely it was because it seemed to me that if I said no it would mean I was scared. And so, I agreed to take the dare and give hypnotic regression a try.

Several months passed after my conversation with Cathy before I finally made an appointment with her colleague. Even though I had told her at the party I would try regressive hypnosis, I didn't. By the next day, being more clearheaded and logical, I dismissed the idea as a silly waste of time and just forgot about it. I probably never would have gone through regressive hypnosis except that every time I ran into Cathy, she would ask if I had made the appointment yet. Cathy and I weren't that close and I didn't know if this was just her way of broaching the distance between captain and patrol officer (detective in the Indianapolis Police Department is a position and not a rank) or if she really wondered if I had or not. However, each time I said I hadn't made the appointment, my reasons seemed to sound a little less convincing. Tired of making excuses, I finally called her colleague and made an appointment.

Almost immediately, I began feeling nervous and anxious about keeping the appointment. I knew a considerable amount about hypnosis because therapists sometimes used it on patients to dredge up forgotten childhood-abuse memories, and it had also been used in police interrogation for some time with conflicting results and with varying acceptance by the courts. The police occasionally had crime-scene witnesses hypnotized in order to recall events from their deep memory they couldn't remember normally. Many in the criminal justice field, though, saw this technique, like regressive hypnosis to regain childhood-abuse memories, as less than reliable.

I did know, however, through my acquaintance with the hypnosis used by the police, that people under hypnosis do not lose control of themselves and are not under the power and domination of the hypnotist, as so many stage hypnotists want their audiences to believe. So losing control wasn't what made me feel anxious and nervous. It was just the opposite. I felt sure that, being much too strong-willed, I couldn't be hypnotized and that I would instead spend a very uncomfortable hour with a person who would try to convince me I was hypnotized when I knew I wasn't.

On a Tuesday afternoon after work, I finally drove up to the psychologist's office. Dr. Mariellen Griffith's office, I discovered, sat in a cluster of old buildings on the far north side of Indianapolis, a cluster built long before the area had become heavily populated, and which probably at one time had been occupied mostly by dentists and doctors. But the neighborhood now had dozens of newer buildings and office complexes where the dentists and doctors must have moved to, because the complex that housed Dr. Griffith's office contained mostly insurance agencies and small company offices.

I pulled my car into the parking lot fifteen minutes early and then sat there trying to decide how I was going to handle what I had become convinced was going to be a very uncomfortable time. I could see myself sitting in the office and trying to be polite as Dr. Griffith swung a watch or some type of amulet in front of me, or whatever hypnotists did. She would tell me how sleepy I was getting. But I wouldn't be getting sleepy. Instead, I would be getting bored and feeling ridiculous. The whole meeting, I just knew, was going to be very uncomfortable.

But I had made the appointment, and there was no way I could face Cathy and tell her that, after making the appointment, I didn't go through with it, that I had welshed on the dare. That would make it look as if I was scared of the truth. There is a hierarchy in police departments, with a captain near the top (captain was the highest merit rank possible at the police department, with the higher ranks being appointed and temporary). A police captain is not frightened by something as silly as hypnotism. And so, I made the decision right then that I would see this whole thing through. I would cooperate as much as I could with Dr. Griffith, and give it my very best effort. Cathy would not be able to accuse me of not trying.

And so finally, taking a deep breath, I turned off the car, and walked into the rather dark and, I thought, depressing building. I wandered the hallways for a few moments before discovering that Dr. Griffith shared a common reception area with several other offices. Giving my name to the receptionist, I took a seat and picked up an old copy of *Time*.

Several minutes later, the receptionist ushered me into Dr. Griffith's office, a rather dark room with the standard patient's couch, a chair next to the couch, and a wooden desk that looked as though it had probably been old when Freud was practicing. Dr. Griffith, a tall and willowy woman with an unusual, almost musical, voice, must have sensed my reluctance and nervousness because she seemed to try to put me at ease right away with a smile and a gracious welcome.

"Please sit down," Dr. Griffith said after our introduction, pointing to the couch, while she took a seat in the chair next to it. She then asked me a number of questions, and I talked for a few minutes about myself and my family. I wanted to be polite, so I didn't tell her that I was only there on a dare, though I suspected Cathy might have done so. Dr. Griffith seemed particularly interested in my job as a police captain and asked me a number of questions about it. Finally, though, she looked at me with a smile and asked, "So, what is it you think you need help with?"

After a bit of hemming and hawing, I told her that I didn't really have any problems I needed to work on. I just thought that past-life regression sounded interesting and I wanted to try it.

Dr. Griffith didn't seem to be a bit put off or surprised by my statement, yet said that before we started she needed to explain a few things about hypnotic regression. For the next few minutes she described how in my subconscious mind there resided my "higher self," a sort of spirit who would guide me throughout our hypnotic session, allowing me to see only the parts of my past that it felt would help me in this life. She then described how while in regression I would be surrounded by a white light that would protect me. I struggled not to smile. I had been a police officer for many years and had faced danger many times. I had faced crazed people with butcher knives and guns; I had faced rabid dogs; and I had once found myself trapped in a narrow hallway with a man pointing a shotgun at my chest and screaming he was going to kill me. As a police officer, I had seen the many, many horrible things human beings do to each other, and so I didn't think I could see anything while under hypnosis that would frighten or upset me. Nonetheless, I nodded politely and listened.

CHAPTER TWO

Dr. Griffith took a deep breath and then leaned forward, telling me to get comfortable and we'd get started. I had been told when I made the appointment that I could bring along my own tape recorder, and so I had. I felt the real need to be able to prove, if necessary, that I had given the session my best shot. I reached over and snapped on the "record" button, then waited for Dr. Griffith to begin swinging something in front of my face and telling me how sleepy I was getting. But she didn't. Instead, she simply told me to close my eyes and describe to her the den in my home. I did this for several minutes, telling her about the arrangement of the furniture, what hung on the walls, the position of the bookcases, and so on.

"Now find the spot in your den that you think is the most comfortable, and imagine yourself sitting there," she told me.

I have an overstuffed blue chair that I sit in while reading, and in my mind I saw myself sitting there.

"Now picture your higher self coming into the room to greet you," Dr. Griffith said.

I did that too, though as I sat on the couch with my eyes closed I couldn't help but wonder what the hell I was doing there, particularly when she asked me what my higher self was wearing. How the hell would I know? This was her daydream. I couldn't see anything. But I really wanted to prove to Cathy that past-life regression wasn't real, so I knew I needed to give the session a fair shot.

"White," I answered. "A long white gown." Wasn't that what all spirits wore?

"Can you see what color of eyes your higher self has?"

"Brown," I said. Since I have brown eyes, I figured my higher self would have to have them too.

"Your higher self is standing there and asking if you're ready to go on a trip. It is telling you that it will guide you and protect you on your trip."

Oh Lord, I thought as I tried to maintain a facial expression of seriousness, I can't believe I'm doing this.

"I'm going to count backwards now from ten," she continued, "and with each number you'll become more and more relaxed. Ten."

At this point, it took all of my willpower to keep from opening my eyes and telling her that we were simply wasting each other's time. But I didn't open my eyes, and I didn't say anything.

"You're … going … deeper," Dr. Griffith said, spacing each word and drawing out her sentences. "Nine. More and more relaxed. Eight. Deeper and deeper. More relaxed. Seven. More and more relaxed. Six. Deeper. Five. Deeper and deeper."

Dr. Griffith's voice, I found, began to take on more and more the tone of a stage hypnotist, the kind who says, "You're getting sleeeeeeeepy, very sleeeeeeeepy." But I wasn't feeling anything except for the rather hard couch beneath my buttocks and the floor under my feet.

"Four. Relaxed." Each of Dr. Griffith's words now seemed to take seconds. "Three. More and more relaxed. Two. Deeper. One. Now you're more relaxed. Much more relaxed."

Actually I wasn't relaxed. I was tense from feeling and, I'm sure, looking like a simple-minded fool for getting myself involved in this. A police captain sitting with his eyes closed and waiting to be transported back to a past life. I knew I should never have done this.

"Now look around your den and see the furniture and the books. See your higher self standing in front of you. You feel relaxed and safe and comfortable."

Trying to be cooperative, I pictured my den in my mind, along with someone who looked like me dressed in a white robe and standing in front of my blue chair.

"Now I want you to go back to your college graduation. See it in your mind and describe it to me."

I began telling Dr. Griffith about my college graduation, having to concentrate hard since it had been almost twenty years, yet I was still doing my best to describe it to her.

"Now I want you to go back to high school," she said when I'd finished describing my graduation from college. "See if you can imagine in your mind an incident that occurred during high school, and describe it to me."

I told her about a high school dance I had attended. It wasn't a dance I had attended with a girl, but one in which I had been asked to help with the lighting. At the time, that sounded neater than going with a girl since it meant I would be allowed to climb around on the catwalk high above the gym floor.

"Okay," she said when I finished, "now go back to junior high. Tell me about something that happened then, and try to really imagine it in your mind."

That one I had to think about for a bit, but a memory finally surfaced, and I told her about an incident that had occurred in a history class when our teacher told everyone she didn't like Fidel Castro, who had just come to power in Cuba about a year earlier. I remembered the incident because I found the teacher's reasoning unusual. She didn't say she disliked Castro because he was a communist, a dictator, or even a bad man. She said she didn't like him because he wore a beard.

"Now let's go down to elementary school," Dr. Griffith said, "and see if you can get a picture in your mind of an event that occurred then."

This was getting tougher and tougher, and it took a minute or so before I finally recalled and described to her an event during grade school that I felt was an act of religious prejudice by one of my teachers. The parents of a young girl in my fifth-grade class wouldn't sign an approval slip for their daughter to attend religion classes at a nearby church. From that point on, the teacher seemed to single the girl out and treat her badly.

"And now go back to the earliest childhood memory you have. Picture it in your mind and describe it to me."

I tried to anticipate what Dr. Griffith's next question would be as I described to her my earliest memory at the age of about three or four. It would be difficult not to smile if she next asked me about womb memories or memories from a past life. I wouldn't be able to tell her anything, and I certainly wasn't going to make anything up.

When I finished describing my earliest memories, I again began feeling anxious because, just as I had suspected before coming there, absolutely nothing hypnotic had happened to me so far. I wasn't in any kind of trance. And I certainly wasn't under any kind of control by Dr. Griffith. I was just tired and bored. I was sitting with my eyes closed on a very stiff couch, and I could hear street noises outside the window to my right. My hands, folded in my lap with my fingers clasped, began to hurt a bit, and the rather hard couch made my buttocks ache, but I didn't move my fingers or my buttocks. Also, sitting for so long with my eyes closed made my eyelids feel sticky, but I didn't move them either.

"Okay, now I want you to imagine what it was like before you were born. I want you to imagine yourself asking your parents what they wanted from you as a son. Imagine asking them what they wanted you to be."

In spite of my willpower, I smiled a bit. Dr. Griffith wouldn't be a good interrogator, I thought. It was much too easy to anticipate her next question. And anyone who can do that can prepare for it. But still, I told her what I thought my parents had probably wanted of me and then answered her next question, which was, what had I expected and wanted from my parents? These weren't memories, however, just my thoughts and opinions.

"And now I want you to imagine your parents fading away," Dr. Griffith said. "You are back with your higher self, who has put a circle of white light around you that will protect you from anything you see or experience."

I still couldn't understand what it was she thought I might see that would be so frightening, but I nodded slowly as I tried to imagine it.

"And now imagine that your higher self is taking you to a balloon. A large balloon filled with air. He says for you to climb into this balloon and you'll go back together to your earliest memories, to the first time you were on this earth. Now climb into the balloon and fly high in the sky. See yourself floating up higher and higher in the sky. The balloon is warm and comfortable, and you feel safe. Do you see the color of the balloon?"

I could see a round, purple blob on the insides of my closed eyelids, which I suspected came from the light filtering in through the window to my right. "Yeah, it's purple," I answered.

"Purple is the color of royalty," Dr. Griffith said in her musical voice. "Now see yourself dropping down. Dropping down to earth. Tell me what you see."

I didn't see anything. The purple blob was still there, but I sure didn't see anything else. "I can't see anything."

"Can you see any lights below you?"

Actually, I could see what appeared to be lights down at the bottom of my closed eyelids, but I knew it was simply glare off of the tile floor. Still, I wanted to be cooperative. "Yes, I can see lights down below."

"Would you like to go down there?"

"Uh, sure."

"Okay then, now slowly descend. See yourself slowly going down."

I tried, but all I could see was just the purple blob and the lights at the bottom of my closed eyelids. Interestingly, the lights didn't look so much like glare off of the floor as they did little points, though I still dismissed them as being simply a reflection. "Nothing's happening."

"But you'd like to go down there, wouldn't you?"

"Sure."

"Okay then, what you need to do is to reach up. There is a control over your head. Reach up and pull on it and it will bring the balloon down."

I tried to imagine myself doing this, but all I saw was the same purple blob and the lights below. "Nothing's happening," I repeated, now more positive than ever that hypnotic regression was nothing more than people who admired and therefore wanted to please their therapists, people who would tell their therapists that they see anything they're asked to see. I felt certain that Dr. Griffith hadn't run into too many honest people like me, and I suspected that right about then she probably wanted to reach over and slap me. But by the tone of her voice, I could tell I didn't seem to perturb her.

"Now imagine that your higher self is helping you take the balloon down."

We went through this at least a dozen more times in different variations, but still nothing changed for me.

"Okay," Dr. Griffith said finally, not even a hint of irritation in her still soft, musical voice, "your higher self is telling you that this is not a place you want to stop. He will take you somewhere else. He will take you someplace where it's warm and sunny. Now see the higher self take control of the balloon and off you go. The higher self is guiding the balloon. He is taking you to a place where you will want to stop. And off you fly."

Dr. Griffith paused for a moment, then continued. "Your higher self says, 'Look, there is a mountain. A very tall mountain. This is a place I like to come to. Let's fly over there. This is a place we can rest.' Now imagine yourself coming to this mountain. Can you see the mountain?"

I had been sitting on the couch without moving for what I figured had to be at least a half hour. My buttocks ached, my back was beginning to hurt, my fingers (still clasped tightly together) had gone numb, and my eyelids felt so sticky I was certain they were now glued shut. My body, I figured, with so much discomfort, must have told my mind that it was tired of nothing happening. Suddenly, my imagination began working. Without even trying, I could see in my mind the foggy picture of a large mountain.

"Yes... I... I can see it," I said, though knowing it was just my imagination.

"Now the higher self slowly lets the air out and brings you down to the top of this mountain. And slowly you descend with him because you know this is a safe place. Slowly you descend until very softly you land. There is a little house on the top of the mountain. Now visualize the house and describe what you see."

My mind and body, I figured, must have been not only tired, but completely exhausted, because all at once I could see a blurry log cabin, but with the logs going vertically rather than horizontally, and I saw what looked like flowers growing on the roof of the cabin. I described the building as best I could. Still, though, I knew what I was seeing was only a daydream, just a blurry picture in my mind.

"And as you walk inside this building," Dr. Griffith said once I had finished describing it to her, "tell me what you see."

"It's empty," I said, seeing nothing but dark, vague, empty rooms in my mind. "Just a big empty building." I figured the reason I saw nothing but empty rooms was because this was her daydream, not mine. She had thought up the cabin, not me. I began to suspect that these daydreams, at the therapist's suggestion, were what people must believe are past-life memories. I began to suspect that past-life regression was just an exhausted body's imagination, brought up to please the therapist.

"Now turn to your higher self. He has the power to change this into a warm, cheery place. He can materialize anything you need. See if you can imagine him materializing a table full of food."

I could, though barely, and told her, "It looks like a Thanksgiving meal."

"Lots of good food to eat. You may refresh yourself. Eat and drink as much as you like."

Dr. Griffith paused for probably a minute or so, and then continued. "And now that you've refreshed yourself, your higher self says, 'Let's go down into the valley.' And as you walk out of the cabin, you can see there are steps carved into the stone. There are twelve steps that go down into the valley. I'm going to count these steps as we slowly go down into the valley. There are just twelve steps and your higher self is going to be with you. Twelve … eleven …."

In my mind I could see the hazy picture of some steps, and I tried to imagine myself going down them.

"Ten … nine … eight … seven … six …," she said. With each number, Dr. Griffith's voice became softer and the words longer. "Fiiive … foooour …" She paused for a moment. "Thrrrrree … twwwwwwo … onnnnnnne. Okay, now look around and tell me what you see."

I hardly heard what Dr. Griffith said when she finished counting because something happened, something so bizarre and startling that I would have screamed in surprise if I hadn't already lost my breath.

The Prehistoric Man

I stood in a valley. I don't mean I just imagined or daydreamed that I stood in a valley or that I just saw a valley in my mind. I was there. This wasn't something I had simply visualized for Dr. Griffith's sake. I was there. I could see the trees and thick underbrush all around me. I could hear the chirping of birds in the nearby branches and could feel the tingling breeze of a slight wind blowing in my face. The experience felt a little, but only a very little, like one of those waking dreams I've had a few times in my life, dreams that came when I wasn't quite asleep, yet not totally awake either, but rather when my awareness was just skimming across the surface of my subconscious mind, alternately dipping in and out of it.

I didn't feel frightened by what was happening, just stunned. The change had occurred so abruptly, it seemed as if I had suddenly walked through a door and into another world. One moment I had been sitting in a dim office trying to visualize a scene for Dr. Griffith, and the next moment I stood in a valley with bright sunlight all around me.

Yet, while what I was experiencing did vaguely resemble a waking dream, it also appeared very different from one in that it didn't have the surrealistic quality of dreams. The setting I found myself in was much more lifelike and vivid—so lifelike and vivid that I felt strangely uneasy. I had never experienced anything like this before, and I wasn't sure what was happening. Still, that day, as I found myself seeming to be physically standing in a valley somewhere, I knew that in reality I sat on a couch in Dr. Griffith's office. I could still feel the various discomforts I'd been experiencing from having sat for so long without moving, and I could still hear Dr. Griffith when she moved in her chair, along with sounds on the street outside the window to my right. Yet, at the same time, I also stood in a heavily forested valley.

Yet, even though I realized that this was all just some trick the hypnosis was playing on my mind, and nothing more, I still felt an uneasiness because, unlike a dream or even imagination, there were no blurry, foggy edges to what I saw. Everything around me looked sharp, clear, and extraordinarily lifelike. I could see the gorge of the valley ahead of me, and I could see the thick forest running up the steep slopes on either side. As I looked around, I could see the leaves on the trees moving in the wind and I could feel the breeze on my face. But how, I wondered, could I feel the wind in a closed office? Was it just the air-conditioning in Dr. Griffith's office? If so, I hadn't noticed it before.

However, what really set this experience apart was that I had control of it. I could look around. This wasn't like a dream, in which whatever events were occurring controlled what I saw and where my attention was drawn. I could control this experience. I could decide where I wanted to look and what I wanted to look at. And while most dreams have some type of action going on that propels the plot, in this case nothing was happening other than a slight breeze blowing. I was simply standing alone in a very beautiful valley. There was nothing else happening. It occurred to me that this was like some type of virtual reality game, except that the landscape didn't have a cartoon feel to it. Instead, it looked vividly realistic. But, I realized, like virtual reality, it only looked as if the world I found myself standing in was genuine, while I knew it really wasn't. In my mind, I may have thought I was standing in a valley. I may have thought I could feel the breeze in my face. However, I knew it was just a trick brought on by the hypnosis.

"You're now down in the valley," Dr. Griffith said. "What do you see?"

"Trees," I answered, "lots of trees." The scene shifted suddenly, and I turned and looked to my right, seeing that I was now walking along the bank of a small brook. I could also see that I was now in a different part of the valley. It suddenly occurred to me that I apparently didn't have total control of what was happening after all because I hadn't done anything to bring about this change in location, or had even wanted it. It had just happened, like a scene shifting in a movie. "There's a brook running through the valley to my right," I told Dr. Griffith while looking around in amazement. I could still see the leaves moving with the slight breeze that was blowing and could still feel its coolness on my face. "But there's lots of thick trees. Trees all the way up both sides of the valley."

"Now look down at yourself and see what you're wearing," Dr. Griffith said.

I looked down and saw a pair of dirty, gnarly feet and two hairy legs. Above that I seemed to be wearing some type of dark fur that appeared to be filthy and matted. "I'm wearing some kind of animal skin," I told her. I glanced back down and saw that I carried what looked like a piece of a large tree limb in my left hand, a piece shaped like a very shallow "V." I could feel that it was a heavy, solid piece of wood. "And I'm carrying what looks like a piece of a tree limb."

"Are you a male or female?"

"A man," I answered immediately, not sure where the knowledge or answer came from, but somehow knowing this to be true.

"Now see yourself looking around, and see if you can find any shelter."

All at once, a recognition and awareness of where I was came crashing into my mind like a speeding car coming through a showroom window. I knew exactly where I was! This apparent recognition of the valley startled me because it felt as though I were suddenly using two separate parts of my mind at the same time. The part of my mind that I was familiar with, the part that had generated and contained my thoughts ever since I'd had awareness, knew that I had never seen this valley before, but at the same time it felt as if a long-closed door buried in the deepest reaches of my mind had creaked opened and was letting little thoughts and bits of recognition slip out. The knowledge that escaped through this door told me that I recognized this valley as my home, and that it had been my home for a long time.

"There's a cave up the hill on my right," I told Dr. Griffith. I looked up the steep slope of the valley to a rocky outcropping. The newly opened part of my mind told me that the rocky outcropping was my home. What I saw as I stood staring up the side of the valley looked familiar, but only in the context of this previously unused portion of my mind—not in the memory of Bob Snow, who now seemed to be mostly a passive observer of the events I was seeing.

"And does this look like a safe place?"

"It's where I live," I said, stunned because I hadn't known I was going to say that. It felt as though all at once I no longer had control of my voice, as if my words were instead being controlled by this newly opened part of my brain, a part I had never known existed. The words that now came off of my lips seemed to bypass my conscious mind. And yet, all of this time, while I was walking through the valley, recognizing the landmarks, and saying things about them, I could still feel the pain in my hands, back, and buttocks; and I could still hear the noises that came into Dr. Griffith's office.

"Now walk into the cave and tell me what you see."

Instantly, I found myself standing just inside the cave's mouth. I didn't have to walk there from the spot where I had been standing a moment before, but again, like a movie changing scenes, I simply found myself there. And while I knew it was impossible, I thought for a moment that I could smell the musty and disgusting odor of years of unsanitary habits. This truly stunned me because, unlike the wind I had felt, I couldn't come up with an explanation for the smell.

"I see light," I said finally. "There's a hole in the roof of the cave. And there's water. Water runs through it."

"Do you have a mate?"

"No," I answered immediately, again somehow aware of this information, but at the same time feeling a deep sadness about it.

"Do you have a name?"

This question, to whatever part of my mind now controlled what I was experiencing, didn't seem to make any sense. "No. I'm just me."

"Now look outdoors. Is it spring or summer?"

Rather than instantaneous movement, this time I turned and walked just outside the cave entrance. The cave, I found, sat high up on the side of the valley, and an open, rocky space separated it from the thick forest of the valley below. The leaves on the trees looked full and thick, the underbrush beneath them appearing almost impenetrable. "It's summer. Everything is really green."

"Do you have any idea what the date is?"

Again a question with no sense to it. "No."

"Do you have any idea of your age? How old are you?"

"I don't think I'm very old."

Dr. Griffith paused for a moment as I continued to look down at the valley, still stunned by what was happening and amazed at what I was seeing. Where had this vision come from? I wondered. What was the source of this illusion that made me think I was standing above a lush, beautiful landscape that I thought I recognized? Had I seen this valley long ago but just forgotten it? Was this simply a long-buried memory dredged up from my subconscious mind? The vividness of what I was experiencing still stunned me. No matter what I thought about the reality of regressive hypnosis, something amazing was happening.

And yet, while I was without a doubt having one of the most unique and bizarre experiences of my life, I didn't sense any fear. I didn't feel any need for the white light or my spirit guide to protect me. Actually, I found that I was beginning to enjoy it. The experience wasn't frightening, and it wasn't even unnerving any longer because I knew that in reality I wasn't in a valley—no matter how vivid it appeared, I knew I was still sitting in Dr. Griffith's office. I knew that everything I was seeing and experiencing was simply a trick that the hypnosis was playing on my mind. Furthermore, while I may have earlier doubted that it could be done, I realized I must be in a fairly deep hypnotic trance. What I was seeing had to be just some forgotten memories that the hypnosis had dredged up. It couldn't be real, though I had to admit that the hypnotic trance certainly gave the memories a very realistic feel.

A car honked on the street outside the window to my right, but it seemed far away, as did the pain in the various parts of my body. I found myself totally absorbed and fascinated by what was happening and decided to just let it flow wherever it wanted and simply enjoy it. It was, I thought with a little twinge of guilt, sort of like a drug trip without the drugs. It was the type of thing that people took LSD to experience, yet without the dangers, and without being illegal. I felt very confident that if, as Dr. Griffith had seemed to think I might, I suddenly found myself facing dredged-up memories that scared me or memories that I didn't want to face, I could just open my eyes and stop it. Regardless of what stage hypnotists may wish the audience to believe, I knew I still had complete and total control, not Dr. Griffith, albeit control with parts of my brain I hadn't known existed. But still it was my brain. Dr. Griffith was simply a guide. I was the one in charge of what was happening, and could continue the vision or stop it at my wish. So, since nothing bad was happening, I decided to just continue to enjoy the vision of standing at the cave's mouth, staring down at the thick green of the valley below. As I looked around, I didn't see any animal life, but I somehow knew, again at a deep, previously untapped level of my brain, that the valley teemed with all types of animals, some of them very dangerous.

"And now I want you to go forward until you reach the time you are about to die," Dr. Griffith said, clearing her throat and shifting again in the chair. Her voice and the sound of her movement seemed to come out of the air around me as I stood looking at the valley.

The lush, green valley below suddenly faded out, and when the scene around me came back into focus I found myself no longer in the body I had been in earlier, but now somehow floating ten feet or so above it. Below me I could see a thin, dirty, little man lying on the cave floor. He was covered with animal skins, shivering and coughing. "I'm sick and I'm dying," I said, once more having the words just roll off of my lips without passing first through my conscious mind. "There's no one with me. I'm all by myself."

"What do you feel?"

"I feel cold," I said, wondering why I said that or how I knew it since I wasn't in the body any longer, but instead was floating above it. In this state I couldn't, as I had a few moments before, sense or feel anything that the body below me experienced.

Dr. Griffith again paused for a moment as I watched the little man hugging himself under the animal skins and trying to get warm, but still shivering. Every few moments he would cough with an intensity that I somehow knew was tremendously painful.

"And now I want you to pass out of this life. I want you to rise up out of … "

"I'm all alone," I blurted out so suddenly it startled me. It was as if a small voice whispered words to me through the newly opened door in my mind, and they immediately went to my lips. But I also somehow knew that what I was about to say was a very important point, and that I had to talk about it. "There's no one with me," came the words from deep inside my mind. "I'm all by myself." I felt an urgent, powerful need to express this, to say these things. But then, all at once, I seemed to catch a momentary glimpse of what was behind the newly opened door in my mind. Experiencing loneliness had been the reason for this existence. The point of this life had been to learn what it was like to be completely and totally alone. "I didn't have anyone. Just me. All alone."

"Now I want you to pass out of this life," Dr. Griffith repeated. "I want you to rise up and look for the light."

Suddenly, my viewpoint left the dying man and I found myself outside the cave, still floating ten feet or so above the ground. Below me, I could see the approach to the cave and the trees of the valley packed so tightly together they looked like one huge piece of vegetation. Then all at once, without any warning or sign that I was about to move, I found myself floating high above the valley.

"And now you're in the soul state," Dr. Griffith said. "Do you see a light?"

"Yes," I said, looking up and seeing an intensely bright light seeming to hover over the valley.

"Go toward the light. You will be safe there."

"This was a bad life," I found myself again unexpectedly saying as I headed toward the light. "A bad life."

"What did you learn from this life?"

The answer seemed to zing onto my tongue as if on springs. "That it's not good to be alone. That you need someone." I felt a strange sense of satisfaction at expressing this, as though it explained everything I had just experienced. But at the same time I realized that my experience, even though I had earlier thought of it as merely long-forgotten memories dredged up from my subconscious mind, just didn't seem to fit. In my life as Bob Snow, I had never experienced real loneliness like the caveman had. I had always had a spouse or my family nearby. Where had the idea of experiencing loneliness come from? Dr. Griffith hadn't mentioned it. It had simply come up with the vision I was experiencing.

Dr. Griffith paused for a few moments, as if to let what I had experienced and said sink in, then continued. "Okay, now I want you to go forward in time. Go forward until you find a life when you did have someone important to you."

All at once, as I neared the bright light, the scene around me faded, but just for a few seconds.

The Artist

I could hear a car revving its engine on the street outside the window of Dr. Griffith's office as the scenes I had witnessed with the cave man faded into a sort of gray fog. My buttocks no longer hurt. They had instead now gone totally numb and were beyond feeling. The pain had moved out of them and up into my lower back. I continued, as I had since I first sat down, to keep my hands tightly clasped together in my lap, and they likewise had gone numb. I knew that I needed to stretch and flex to get the blood flowing throughout my body again, but I didn't dare move because I feared it would stop everything I was seeing. I'm not sure why, but I felt convinced that the intense stress I was under was driving the hypnosis, and that if

I moved any part of my body the scenes would fade away like a late-morning dream, and I wouldn't be able to bring them back. I knew I was having a once-in-a-lifetime experience, and I didn't want it to end.

And yet, while I was having an amazing experience, I kept telling myself that it wasn't real, no matter how vivid. It had to be simply my mind dredging up old memories, or perhaps bits of movies and books, from my subconscious and recasting them into a story line that fit what Dr. Griffith had asked of me. Still, I felt uncomfortable with that explanation because everything appeared so vivid and lifelike. It was as if I was actually there. And though I knew it was impossible, it seemed as if I could even smell, hear, and feel in the visions. They were that realistic. It was unbelievable. It was like discovering the most fascinating ride imaginable at an amusement park, and I wanted more of it.

I also knew that there was no doubt I was in some kind of hypnotic state. Only a deep hypnotic trance, I assumed, would allow my subconscious mind to take over so completely. Only deep hypnosis could allow my subconscious mind to present these scenes so vividly and logically reconstructed that they would appear to be real memories of a past life. But while I recognized this fact, being in a hypnotic state didn't feel the way I had thought it would. I didn't feel groggy or like a zombie. I felt completely clearheaded and in control. I knew I maintained complete command of my actions and could do or not do as Dr. Griffith asked. Several times she had suggested things that the story line my subconscious mind was apparently inventing wasn't ready for yet, and it ignored her and went its own way. I also knew that I could leave the hypnotic state at any time simply by opening my eyes. But I didn't want to. This had become, without the slightest doubt, the most fascinating experience of my life, a sort of makeshift virtual reality. I couldn't wait to see what my subconscious mind would send up next. And while I figured I would probably never know whether these were real scenes from this life simply dug up from years past, re-ordered, and given back to me, or just wild imagination, I didn't care. I wanted to see more. Yet the fog around me stayed thick for several moments, and I wondered if my subconscious mind couldn't find anything else to dredge up that would fit the story line suggested by Dr. Griffith.

However, after a few more moments, as I stayed sitting without movement on the couch, a scene began to appear again, at first blurry, but then finally sharpening enough to become as clear as the earlier scene in the valley. I found myself now on a city street, but not a street from today or even from the recent past. It appeared to me more like the late nineteenth century. I could see gas lamps along the sidewalk and carriages being pulled by horses.

"I see a street," I said, realizing that I was again inside a body.

"Describe the street."

"It's in a city."

"Can you tell what year or century this is?" Dr. Griffith asked.

"Late eighteen hundreds. There's gas lights and lots of horses."

"What are you wearing?"

I looked down at myself. "I'm wearing a fancy shirt and jacket."

"What kind of shoes are you wearing?"

"They're real shiny. And I'm carrying a cane. But I'm not an old man. It's like a fancy cane, more of a status symbol than a crutch. And I'm walking down the street."

"Where are you going?"

Again, data slipped out of my subconscious, totally bypassed my conscious mind, and spilled out of my mouth, surprising me when I said, "I'm walking to meet someone. It's a woman."

"Describe this woman."

"She's waiting for me on the corner. She's very beautiful."

"What's her name?"

For some reason the name proved difficult to pull up. It seemed to be a name I ought to know very easily, but I found that my subconscious mind didn't want to give it to me. "Amanda," I answered finally, though right away feeling uncomfortably certain that this wasn't exactly right. I felt her name probably sounded something like that, but not quite Amanda.

"And now you see yourself at your destination," Dr. Griffith said. "Where did you go?"

"She took my arm and we walked down the street together."

"And where did you go?"

"We're just walking down the sidewalk." I looked around at the scene I was seeing and noticed that the street appeared crowded with people and carriages. It seemed to be summer because I could feel the heat of the sun on me.

"What do you see or do as you walk down the sidewalk together?"

"It's a real busy street, but we don't seem to notice. She seems real happy and so do I."

"What's Amanda wearing?" Dr. Griffith asked.

"It's red. And it's got like this big bustle in the back. We're not just walking. We're headed somewhere."

"You now see yourself at your destination," Dr. Griffith instructed. "Where are you?"

"We've stopped to eat somewhere. It's outside. It's on the sidewalk somewhere." I looked around and could see several dozen diners sitting at the black metal tables around Amanda and me, but no one seemed to be paying any attention to us.

"Now see yourself sitting at the table. What have you ordered?"

"She wants some kind of special water. And I order myself a glass of wine."

"Now go forward in time and see if you married this girl. Did you marry Amanda?"

Gray clouds rolled in and blocked out the scene. "No, I don't think so. I can't see her anymore." Suddenly, a sentence burst out of me, though again, I don't know where this information came from. "My name's Jack."

"Okay, your name's Jack. Now go forward until you see Amanda again."

Seeming to have more difficulty than before, my vision very slowly switched from the gray clouds to the hallway of what appeared to be an apartment building. "I see an old building. I'm inside the building with Amanda. She's angry about something."

"What is she angry about?"

"I think it's money. We're married after all. She's angry because I have no money. We're arguing, but I just leave."

"And where do you go?"

The vision shifted again, but this time the new scene didn't become clear as quickly as the others had. I saw myself in a bright, but blurry, room, the light seeming to come from all around, the air of the room feeling stifling hot. I could see the objects in the room, but everything looked a degree or two out of focus. "I'm in a room. It seems like it's full of windows and skylights. It's so bright. I think I'm an artist. There's paintings. The whole place is full of paintings."

"Can you see what kind of paintings they are?"

"I think they're abstract, but I can't see them clearly." The scene finally began to clear, like an out-of-focus movie screen being adjusted, until finally it came into sharp focus. "No, they're not abstract." I could see now that they were paintings of countrysides and lots of portraits. "They're scenes and pictures of people."

"And have any of these paintings been sold?"

"I don't think so. There's an awful lot of paintings here." Suddenly, more information from the hidden source gushed out. "I think this is where I work."

"And so you think you're an artist?" Dr. Griffith asked.

Although I didn't know why, I felt certain the body I was in was that of an artist. "Yes. This is where I work."

"Are you happy?"

"Yes. I'm happy when I paint. But I don't think I'm very successful. There's no money. I'm a good painter though. I'm really a good painter. I truly am. But I just can't make any money."

"Now go forward five years," Dr. Griffith told me, "and tell me what you see."

Like the scene in the artist studio, the change took several moments before it finally cleared and became sharp. "I'm at a party," I said, looking around at the many people standing close to me, everyone smiling and seeming happy. "We're celebrating something. Amanda's here with me too." I could sense that the artist felt immensely proud and was reveling in whatever honor was being bestowed upon him. "I'm the guest of honor at some kind of party. Everyone's congratulating me for something. I don't know what it is, but everyone's congratulating me."

"Are they recognizing you for being an artist?"

"I don't know, but everybody's happy. Amanda's happy."

"And now you are successful?"

"I don't know, but we're all dressed real well."

"And now move ten years forward in time," Dr. Griffith instructed me.

But I didn't. Instead, I hesitated and continued looking around the room, seeing all the people smiling at me. I didn't want to leave. I could sense that this moment was one of the happiest and most important ever for the person whose body I was inhabiting. I wanted to stay around and experience more of the feeling. A person doesn't experience intense happiness that often, and I was enjoying it.

"And now move ten years forward," Dr. Griffith said once more.

Even though I realized I was being foolish, since these weren't real memories and very likely just my imagination, I still didn't want to leave. The body I was inhabiting and everyone around me seemed so happy and joyous. A deep feeling that came from the hidden reservoir in my mind told me that this was one of the peak moments of this body's life, and so I really wanted to stay there for a while and enjoy it. But I left. I wanted to see more. The scene faded, and when the gray clouds around me finally cleared, I found I was now standing outside.

"Where are you now?" Dr. Griffith asked.

"I'm on a large estate, a real large estate. I'm walking through a garden." I could see rows and rows of neatly trimmed hedges and lots of flowers. There were flowers everywhere.

"Is anyone else there with you?"

"No, I'm by myself. I'm walking by myself. I'm sad. I'm looking at the flowers and the plants but I'm not paying any attention to them. I'm thinking about something else." I could sense a deep feeling of depression that seemed to grip my body like a smothering black cloud.

"Okay now, move forward again in time. Now see yourself moving forward," Dr. Griffith said. "Your body has died. See your soul leaving your body. And now look down and tell me what lessons you have learned from this life."

"We should have had children," I said almost immediately. "We were happy, but we didn't have any children. I don't think Amanda could have children."

"What else did you learn?"

"If you work hard enough, you can be successful. I didn't give up. I knew I could paint. I could paint well. But it took so long."

"Okay now, go up to the light. Fly up into the light."

All at once, I could feel myself rising upward through the roof of a building and then high into the sky over a huge city. It was night and the city lit the land for what looked like miles in every direction. But contrary to Dr. Griffith's instructions, I didn't fly up into the bright light above me. Instead, I left the city and flew through some woods. In this form, unlike when I occupied a body, I had no sense or feeling of the evening's temperature, but I could see that it appeared to be a cold, blustery night. It didn't seem to be winter though. The trees still had their leaves, and I saw no snow or ice. I sensed it instead to be a cold, fall night. A moment later, I found myself out of the woods and looking through the windows on the second or third floor of a large mansion, apparently floating there.

"I can see one of my paintings," I said as I looked through the windows. "It's hanging above a fireplace." A huge fire roared in the fireplace as I stared at the painting. "It's got a big yellow circle in it. Like the sun or something." Even though a large fire burned in the fireplace, I didn't see anyone in the room. "The people must've liked it. The people hung it over their fireplace in a big house. A really big house. I don't think they liked me. But they liked my painting." I studied the brightly colored painting some more. "It's a bottle with fruit around it, and there's a big sun behind it."

"And now, let's move on," Dr. Griffith said. "Move up toward the light and get refreshed." She paused for several moments as I continued, rather than letting myself be drawn up toward the bright light that hovered in the sky, to look through the windows at the painting. Finally, Dr. Griffith said, "Okay, now I want you to go back in time. I want you to choose another lifetime. Go back until you find a lifetime when you were a female."

I had to smile at this instruction. This wasn't going to happen. How could my subconscious mind find any old memories from this life of me as a female? No, I felt pretty certain that this was the moment that was going to disprove past-life regression.

The Greek Girl

A few seconds later, however, I found myself standing in a small clearing in a forest. Immediately, I could tell that this wasn't the forest of the valley I had been in as a prehistoric man. The ground around me looked flat and level for as far as I could see, and the trees appeared to be different types and weren't nearly as thick. Also, I saw none of the underbrush I had seen in the valley. But like the valley earlier, the scene before me appeared vividly clear. Directly in front of me stood a circular, white stone structure, with pillars around the circumference. It didn't look like a building, but more like some type of monument, open in the middle and containing what appeared to be a type of altar.

"I'm in a forest," I said, "and I see … It looks like an altar. But it's outside all by itself."

"Can you sense what you're wearing?" Dr. Griffith asked, her voice now sounding as if, rather than coming from the chair next to me, it was coming out of the air somewhere in the trees nearby, the scenery around me seeming so real.

I looked down and saw a young woman's body, probably a woman in her late teens. "It's white," I said, examining what I was wearing. "It's a dress with hooks on the side. It's like it's not completely around me. It's like two pieces of material with hooks up both sides."

"Can you sense what country you're in?"

"I feel like it's Greece," I answered, not knowing why but feeling certain I was right. I was now becoming used to having information suddenly rush past my conscious mind and onto my lips, and I just let it, no longer surprised when I said something I had no idea I was going to say. "It looks like Greek architecture. It's pillars in a circle."

Dr. Griffith paused for a moment as I stood examining the circular monument, awed by its beauty. The structure was certainly no Parthenon, but in its simplicity it exuded strength and elegance.

After a few more seconds, Dr. Griffith continued. "What is the purpose of this place?"

"It looks like an altar of some type. It's in the woods. There's woods all around it." I could tell from the foliage that it was midsummer.

"And what are you doing there?"

"I'm just standing here. I'm just standing here looking at it."

"How old are you?"

"I'm a teenager."

But then suddenly, the same inner force and knowledge that had washed over me while I stood in the valley and then again in the artist's studio returned, seeming to come from deep inside my brain, and the knowledge and words began spilling out of my mouth. "I work here. I do something here. I bring things down to the altar."

"Do you have a home?" Dr. Griffith asked. "A place to stay?"

I could suddenly see a stone building and a dozen or so other young girls, but not as clearly as I could see the woods and the circular structure. It was as if I was having a memory from the place in the woods where I stood. I could visualize a group of girls sleeping on mats on the cold floor. "It's on top of a hill," I said. "I live with a lot of other girls. We bring things down to the altar every day. It's cold where we live." I could feel the coldness of the stone walls and floor, and a chill went through me as I sat on the couch, making me shiver, even though Dr. Griffith's office seemed to be at a comfortable temperature.

"It's warm there now," Dr. Griffith said. "Warm and comfortable."

Dr. Griffith's statement didn't seem to make any sense to the part of my brain that controlled what I was seeing, because that part of my brain seemed to know that it was often cold where we lived. "No, it's cold," I insisted, still shivering as I sat with my eyes closed on the couch in Dr. Griffith's office.

"What is the purpose of this place where you work?" Dr. Griffith went on. "Do people come here to worship?"

"I don't know. We bring things down to the altar. People come to the altar and we bring things here."

"And who receives these things you bring?"

"I don't know. We just bring things down to the altar and leave them. It's deep in the woods. I can see lots of vines and trees."

"Do you know what century this is?"

"It's a long time ago." Suddenly, more pulses of information began to flash through my mind and toward my lips. I didn't know the year or the time period, but I did suddenly know more about myself. "We're all pretty," I said. "That's why we were picked. And we're all virgins. We're not even allowed to see men. We must stay pure."

"And who is in charge of you?"

"I can see her," I said, the face of an older woman appearing before me. "She's old and has real long brown hair. Dark brown hair. She's mean. She's very stern."

"Okay," Dr. Griffith said. "Now go forward five years in your life. What is it like now?"

The forest around me faded out and a few seconds later a blurry picture came back, then sharpened. "I'm somewhere else," I said, just as amazed as I had been every time I suddenly saw a new scene. "I'm behind something. It looks like a couple of oxen. They're in some kind of yoke. We're in a wagon and we're traveling."

"Who are you traveling with?"

I looked to my left to see who was driving the wagon. "An older man."

"Are you married to him?"

Again, information from behind the newly opened door flowed into my brain, and I spoke without thinking. "No. We're not married. But he's a nice man. He's old. He's really old, but he's a nice man."

"Do you have any children?"

I looked around the wagon again and saw something that stunned me. When I didn't answer her question after a few seconds, Dr. Griffith repeated it, but still I didn't answer for several more seconds. I saw a little girl sitting on the wagon seat to my right, her chubby little legs dangling in front of her. I somehow knew that the little girl was my daughter, and I could feel a sense of love for her. But that wasn't what shocked me. What shocked me was that I recognized her as a person in my present life as Bob Snow. It was my stepdaughter. But it wasn't the teenager I had seen off to high school that morning. It was the small child she had been when I married her mother.

"There's a little girl," I answered finally. "She looks just like me. She is sitting on the seat next to me. She's real pretty."

"Is she happy?"

"Yes, we're both happy," I said. "We're going someplace. We're in a big wagon and we're going somewhere."

"Okay, now you've arrived at your destination," Dr. Griffith instructed. "Where have you stopped?"

"At a farm. He owns a farm."

"Is this your home?"

More knowledge surged into my brain and instantly spilled out of my mouth. "He bought me. I think he bought me, or I was given to him. I belong to him. But he's nice. He's a nice man. But he's also very old. He treats us both good though."

Although I didn't tell Dr. Griffith, I had a thin "memory" pop up in the brain of the woman whose body I inhabited, a memory of me and a man, a memory about not maintaining one of the cardinal requirements for where I had lived and worked: being a virgin. I knew I had been foolish to give up so much on an impulse, because as a consequence of my disobedience, the woman in charge of the girls who tended the altar had given or sold me to the old man. I didn't say anything to Dr. Griffith about this because I felt it would sound foolish since these were not real memories.

"Now move forward in time," Dr. Griffith said, "until the man dies. Now what happens to you?"

"I go back. I go back to the place with the altar. And I bring my daughter. The old man died real soon. He didn't live very long at all. And so I took my daughter back. She's going to be a part of this. She's going to work at the altar just like I did."

"Are you happy about this?"

As I had during the scene in the valley, I caught a momentary glimpse of the information behind the newly opened door in my brain. I knew I wasn't happy about this at all. I realized instead that I was sad about it. I also knew that I was deeply ashamed of what I was doing, because what I was really doing was abandoning my daughter, but I felt I couldn't tell Dr. Griffith that. I couldn't admit that I was abandoning my daughter because it would be easier for me without her. And even though I knew that what I was experiencing wasn't a real memory, I still felt ashamed of myself and didn't want to admit it to Dr. Griffith. It was better, I felt, to just act as though I was doing a good thing. "It's nice for her" was all I said.

Dr. Griffith then asked, "Are you well taken care of?"

"I'm not. She is. I'm going to have to leave her there. I can't stay with her."

"How do you feel about this?"

Although I felt sad and tremendously ashamed, and knew that what I was doing was wrong, I answered, "I'm happy for her. I was happy there, and she will be too."

"So where do you go?"

All at once, with no fog in between this time, I saw a shabby marketplace in a city that sat on the edge of the ocean or a large sea. I no longer inhabited a body, but now seemed to float above the area. "I go to a city. It's really poor. Very poor. I have something to do with fish. I'm old now, and I'm cleaning fish. I think that's my job."

"Were you ever married?"

"No."

"Now look to your death," Dr. Griffith instructed. "What are you dying of?"

Instantly, I found myself back in the body of the woman, now much older. I could feel myself wrapped up tightly in something and suffocating, water all around me. I was fighting, but I was trapped and couldn't breathe. I just kept swallowing salty water. I felt wildly disoriented because, while I couldn't move my arms or legs, at the same time I seemed to be tossed around in the water. It took all of my willpower not to unclasp my hands and grab onto the couch arm. "I think I drown. It has something to do with fish. I think I get caught up in a net or something, and I drown."

"Now see yourself rising up out of your body," Dr. Griffith said. "Being free. Think about this life and tell me what you learned from it."

As I listened to Dr. Griffith's words, I felt my mind deluged with a tidal wave of guilt over the abandonment of my daughter, for leaving her to work at the altar while I went on. I also felt an almost overpowering need to justify what I had done, to make it sound not quite as bad as I knew it really had been. "My daughter would be happier there," I said. "She would have what I had. It was an honor to be able to work there. A real honor to be a part of that. Really, it was an honor. Truly, it was. I gave that to my daughter. I gave her something very important. I knew she would be happier there. I never had anyone in this life, and maybe by doing that, she could. I never had anyone."

"And now let's move on," Dr. Griffith said. "Move up toward the light and get refreshed."

She paused for several moments as I continued to try to rationalize to myself that I hadn't really abandoned my daughter, but had actually given her a better life than I could have if I had kept her. For some reason, it seemed crucially important to me that I believe this, but even so it still rang hollow.

"And now we will move forward to the lifetime previous to your present one. Go to the lifetime just before your present one."

The Artist Again

The vision of the Greek woman's life faded out around me and for several moments all I could see was muted gray clouds. I felt tremendously relieved to be away from that life because the guilt I had felt over abandoning my daughter had been overwhelming, like some type of intense pressure crushing down on me, almost too much to bear. And while I knew that feeling guilty or ashamed was foolish since none of what I was experiencing was true, but rather just my sub-conscious mind building stories from old bits of forgotten information, probably from one of the many abandoned-children runs I had been on as a police officer, I had still felt tremendous guilt about that life.

But then, as the gray clouds cleared, the feeling fell away when the new scene I was in became vividly clear almost right away. I somehow knew that I was viewing the life of the artist again, but now some time before he died. However, rather than floating above, as I had been the last time I had seen the artist's life, I was now back inside the artist's body and also back in my studio.

"I'm painting a portrait of someone," I said, seeing that I had a paintbrush in my hand. A woman, who sat very stiff, with raised, actually hunched, shoulders, posed for me. I could see that she apparently had a hunchback. I didn't know who she was, but I figured she must be someone important if she was willing to pay to have her portrait painted. I gazed at the canvas as I moved the brush over it and saw that the portrait appeared nearly finished.

When I looked around the studio, more knowledge gushed out. "I don't like doing portraits," I told Dr. Griffith. "But I need the money." I could feel an almost desperation in that need for money, as if the painter cared about little else.

"And where are you?" Dr. Griffith asked.

"I'm in my room. I can see the light coming in from above. There's a lady in a long gown, and I'm painting her portrait. I don't like doing portraits."

"What city or country are you in?"

"I don't know. I can't see out the windows above me." I did notice the color of the window frames though. "All the trim on them is painted black."

"Who is the woman you're painting?"

No name or other identifier immediately came to mind. "She's someone important, I think." I really didn't know this to be a fact but only figured she had to be or else I wouldn't be painting a portrait of her. "And I'm painting her, but I don't like doing portraits. I need the money though. I really need the money."

"Now move five years forward in time," Dr. Griffith said. "Where are you?"

The scene changed again and this time I appeared to be in a different building. I was standing next to one of my paintings and having a heated discussion with a man. I could feel an intense anger building inside me. "I'm arguing with someone," I said. "I'm angry because I don't think the light's right for my painting."

"Now go forward again," Dr. Griffith instructed.

I waited as the scene changed once more, and when a new one came into focus I found myself far from the building I had been in a moment before. "There's a big garden, and stone steps that lead up to a house."

"Okay," Dr. Griffith said. "You walk into the house and what do you see?"

I strolled up the stone steps and through the door. "Amanda's playing a piano. It's a big piano. It's got the lid open. She's wearing a yellow dress, a big, full dress."

"What country are you in?"

"I think it's France," I answered.

"Now let's move forward in time again."

The scene went blank, and I drifted into the fog again. However, before another scene appeared, a thought seemed to explode up through my brain and onto my lips with such incredible force that it made me start on the couch. It seemed to be a crucially important thought, even though I didn't know what it meant. "They said she died of a blood clot," I blurted out. "They said it was a blood clot." I felt a huge, heavy sadness suddenly sit on my chest, the kind of sadness people can only feel when they lose someone incredibly important to them. I didn't have any idea who I was talking about. I didn't know if it was my wife or another woman, but I did know that the woman who died of a blood clot had been tremendously important to the artist. Tears felt very close, and a sob began building in my chest. "A blood clot, they said."

Suddenly, the tape recorder I had brought along clicked off with a loud snap, and the hypnotic trance faded away. I had purchased a tape that played for sixty minutes on a side so that I could have an uninterrupted hour of taping. I couldn't believe the time was up, though the numbness of my body told me that I had been sitting without moving for a long time. Still, I wanted to see more, but whatever had controlled my mind had also turned off with the tape recorder.

"And now it's time to come back to the twentieth century," Dr. Griffith said.

But she didn't have to say anything. I was already back, though the scenes I had just witnessed still hung vividly clear in my mind.

CHAPTER THREE

When I tried to open my eyes I found that my eyelids seemed to be stuck together, and I had to blink several times in order to open them fully. My hands, still locked together in my lap, had gone totally numb a long time ago, so I began flexing my fingers in order to get some feeling back into them. As I was doing this, I looked down at my watch. I couldn't believe it. I had been sitting there on the couch, completely still and with my eyes closed, for an hour, almost to the minute. I wouldn't have believed I could do that.

Within a few seconds, when the feeling began coming back into my hands, small prickles of pain started surging outward from my wrists. Continuing to wiggle my fingers, I stood up and arched my back, my buttocks feeling dead. When I did this, I noticed Dr. Griffith smiling at me. I wasn't sure what her smile meant, but I suddenly felt very uncomfortable about what had happened during the last hour and about the things that I had said, my cheeks beginning to warm. I certainly hadn't acted like a police captain. I felt I had acted more like some kind of nut.

I realized my earlier belief that I couldn't be hypnotized had obviously been wrong. Without question, I had been hypnotized, and also without question I had lost at least partial control of my ability to think before I spoke. I still had no idea what had made me say the things I had or where the information had come from, only that during the last hour I had often lost conscious control over what I said. But far worse than worrying about where the words had come from, I knew that for the last hour I had acted like one of those New Age people I'd always rolled my eyes at. I had sat there for an hour and babbled nonsense. So, now that I was no longer hypnotized, I suddenly felt very uncomfortable about my actions of the last hour. And even though the things I had said seemed normal enough when I said them, and had certainly appeared to fit the scenes I was experiencing, they now seemed a bit silly.

Unwilling to meet Dr. Griffith's eyes, I reached over and grabbed my tape recorder, wanting to get out of her office as quickly as I could. I knew with a certainty, now that I was no longer under any kind of hypnosis and had taken a few minutes to review what had happened while I was, that for the last hour I had looked like someone who couldn't control himself. That particularly troubled me because I had been a police officer for many years. Police work is all about control, and I obviously hadn't had much control over myself, or at least not my mouth, for the last hour.

But where, I found myself wondering as I busied myself with the tape recorder so that I wouldn't have to look at Dr. Griffith, had the scenes I saw so vividly come from? My imagination? It had to be, I told myself. Maybe I wasn't as strong-willed as I thought. Maybe somewhere deep inside me, because I had been hypnotized, I wanted to please Dr. Griffith, so I had allowed her suggestions about past lives to cause me to make up those stories out of my imagination. Even as I told myself this, it didn't sound convincing.

Everything I had experienced had been just too vivid and realistic for imagination, I thought, writing the date on the tape as I tried to keep busy until I could get out of there. Much too vivid and realistic. But if what I experienced hadn't been my imagination, what was it? Well maybe, I reasoned, putting the tape into its plastic case, they actually were real memories of sorts, memories not from a past life, but from this life—only memories that I had forgotten. I had thought this while the scenes were occurring, and it made sense. That had to be it! They had to be just dredged-up memories that were pieced together and re-ordered in order to make up a story that would please Dr. Griffith. That had to be it. There was no other explanation. Still, I sensed an almost desperation in this answer, a sense that I needed some rational explanation, actually any rational explanation, to cling to.

"And now that you've looked at these lives," Dr. Griffith said as she turned off her own tape recorder, "can you see how they relate to your present life? Can you see how they apply to what's happening in your life now?"

At that moment I really couldn't. I felt too flustered and confused by what had just happened. And I was too busy trying to convince myself that I had just built up the scenes from forgotten memories.

Still, I knew that everything that had happened during the last hour wouldn't have bothered me nearly as much, even all of the crazy babbling I'd done, if what I'd experienced had the foggy quality of dreams. I would never see Dr. Griffith again, so my embarrassment over what I had said to her would soon pass. But everything I'd seen during the session had been clear and vivid, so clear I could still see the scenes. I mumbled something to Dr. Griffith, I forget exactly what, but something about needing time to think over everything I'd just seen, and that its meaning wasn't clear yet. Dr. Griffith didn't press me, and so I grabbed my tape recorder and tape, and, after writing her a check for $60.00, hurriedly left, the numbness in my buttocks changing to a painful prickling as I headed out of the building. But I didn't really leave. I instead walked out to my car in the parking lot and then sat there for forty-five minutes or so, thinking about what had just happened. There are times in a person's life when events occur that are so profound or so startling that you have to stop and sort them out. You have to stop and decide how they are going to affect you and what your response to them is going to be. This was one of those times.

The images I had seen remained intensely vivid in my conscious mind, and I found that if I closed my eyes I could

still see them. I could still see even the small details just as
clearly as I had while under hypnosis. And so I knew that even
if they had come from my subconscious mind, even if they
had actually been forgotten or suppressed memories, they
were now stored much more accessibly. I could especially
still see the woman with the stiff posture and raised shoulders, the hunchback whose portrait I'd seen myself painting.
I could still see every brushstroke of the portrait. And I could
still see the painting that had hung over the fireplace in the
mansion I'd seen myself visiting as a spirit. If these were just
old memories, why were they so startlingly clear to me now?
Normal memories certainly weren't as clear and vivid. And
if these were simply dredged-up memories recast into a new
story line, where had I seen the two paintings before?

Mulling it over for some time, I finally decided that the
answer would probably come to me one day when I suddenly
remembered where in this life I had seen the paintings (or pictures of the paintings). After a half hour of reviewing and considering everything that had happened, I felt totally confident
that what I had seen simply had to be just forgotten memories:
brought up, pieced together, and then re-ordered. Because, I
told myself, if not, then what just happened went totally against
everything I had always believed in. If I didn't accept that they
were just dredged-up memories, that would mean my whole
belief system would have to be rebuilt, and I would have to
believe in something that went against everything I had ever
learned. No, I told myself, I certainly wasn't prepared to do that

based on such flimsy evidence. Absolutely not. There had to be a more logical explanation. It had to be my mind simply building up stories in order to please Dr. Griffith. That just had to be it. I wasn't going to be one of those people who, because they saw these dredged-up memories, are fooled into believing that what they saw were past lives. And yet, even though I finally convinced myself that I had a logical explanation for what I had seen, I still couldn't shake the feeling that I had just experienced something tremendously profound and important. No matter how much I told myself that everything I had experienced could be explained logically, I still couldn't get over the vividness or the feeling of reality. No, I had to tell myself over and over, my subconscious mind had just found a way to try to accommodate Dr. Griffith.

As I sat in my car, constantly moving around in the seat in order to work the prickling out of my buttocks, I could feel my conviction that I had the right answer slipping and had to tell myself again and again that I had a logical and reasonable explanation for what had just happened. I also had to reassure myself over and over that my belief system was still intact—and that the supposed past lives really didn't fit me anyway. An artist? If that was true, I told myself, then why didn't I have any artistic ability? I had always been an excellent student in school, graduating summa cum laude from Indiana University with degrees in criminal justice and psychology before attending graduate school, majoring in psychology at the University of Wisconsin on a full fellowship. The only time in my entire life I ever received an F on any schoolwork was in an art class. The instructor, who obviously gave no value to sincere and earnest effort, said that I had absolutely no artistic talent at all. But yet, I also had to admit, I had always been interested in art. I wasn't a student of it or anything, and I really didn't know much about it except what I liked and didn't like. I had always been most fond of sixteenth- through eighteenth-century art, and I had always had a strong dislike for impressionism and modern art, which I feel is an attempt to create art without the hard work.

I then recalled how earlier that day, before going to my appointment with Dr. Griffith, I had thought about, if past lives were true, what kind of life would I have led. I could see myself as a soldier, a Native American, or maybe a Viking. But an artist? An altar girl? A cave man? No, these weren't even close to what I had imagined. Not at all. Fortunately, I studied psychology through graduate school, so I knew that the human mind is a strange piece of equipment and full of surprises. I guess my hour with Dr. Griffith proved that.

At last, after forty-five minutes or so of trying to make sense out of what had happened during the session with Dr. Griffith, I finally told myself that no matter how vivid and realistic the scenes were, the only logical explanation that fit was that they were just pieced-together memories from this life. If I believed otherwise, if I believed that these were actually scenes from past lives, then I would also have to admit that all of the New Age people I had rolled my eyes at all of my life were right and I was wrong, that they were the ones who knew the truth and that my belief system was false. No, I couldn't do that. I was a police captain, and I only believed in things I could see and touch, in things I could prove to others.

Finally though, I did call detective Cathy Graban on my car phone. I certainly wasn't ready to say that she was totally, or even partly, right, just that my mind had shown me some very peculiar things. I wasn't sure what they were, I told her, but I could see where people could mistakenly believe that what they had seen were past lives, especially if everyone experienced them as vividly as I did. After a moment of silence when I couldn't think of anything else to say, I thanked her for putting me in contact with Dr. Griffith, and then hung up. Afterward though, I didn't feel satisfied with the conversation. I had sounded, I felt sure, like a person who has just had a profound experience and didn't know how to deal with it. As I drove home, doubts about my explanation kept creeping back into my mind no matter how many times I assured myself that I had determined the only logical and rational explanation for what had happened.

At last, as I pulled into my driveway, I gave up trying to sort it all out. I realized I was giving this incident too much importance. I needed to move on. But as easy as that sounds, no matter how hard I tried to put it out of my mind, the doubts and questions just wouldn't go away. That evening, after much debating about whether I should tell anyone or not, I told my wife what I had experienced. Melanie has a very practical, analytical mind, and I often like to bounce ideas off of her. Since she and Cathy Graban were friends and worked together as child-abuse detectives, she knew why I had gone to see Dr. Griffith. Earlier that day, she told me that she thought I was silly for doing it. She listened politely and patiently as I told her about the session with Dr. Griffith, told her the complete story, but she too was highly skeptical that I had experienced anything other than an overactive imagination or forgotten memories.

I agreed with her, and then dropped the subject. Yet, no matter how much I continued telling myself that I had an explanation for what had happened, the vividness and realistic feel of everything I had experienced still bothered me. Later that night, after my wife had gone to bed, I took the tape of my session into the den and played it, reliving the scenes I had seen. Most were still very vivid in my memory, particularly the colorful still-life painting and the portrait of the hunchbacked woman. Simply by closing my eyes I could see them just as clearly as I had that afternoon: every color, every shading, every brushstroke.

After listening to the tape twice, I told myself again, and I hoped for the last time, that my explanation was right. It was all interesting, but that was it. It had to be just my subconscious mind responding to Dr. Griffith's hypnotic instructions. Even the part about me being a woman had likely come from a movie I had seen once but had just forgotten. Still, I could definitely see how gullible people would believe that these images were genuine past lives. I knew that if it had been a movie, I would certainly have believed that the story took place in a different time period.

But then, I told myself, movies were meant to do that. And, I argued with myself, a person could experience computer-generated virtual reality, and it might all look and feel very lifelike, but that doesn't make it real. And neither did what I saw.

I went back to work the next day at my job as a police captain and tried to put the session with Dr. Griffith out of my mind. But I couldn't. For the next month or so, I would think about it daily—often several times daily. If I watched a television program that took place in any time period other than the twentieth century, I would think about it. If I saw a piece of artwork, I would think about it. And sometimes, nothing in particular would trigger thoughts of my session with Dr. Griffith. But what really disturbed me was that, even a month afterward, if I closed my eyes I could still see the scenes I had experienced and could still see the two paintings vividly. It seemed that no matter how many times I repeated my logical explanation to myself, I still felt uncomfortable about the session. Somehow it just didn't have the feel and texture of pieced-together memories. It had the feel of reality. It had the feel of a total story.

Like most uncomfortable and unresolved things a person tries to shrug off, the session began to enter my mind more and more rather than less and less as time wore on. I would think about it when I was in meetings, when I was reviewing my detectives' case reports, when I was at the scene of a homicide. I even began dreaming about it. At least once or twice a week I would have some dream that involved either Dr. Griffith or the artist's life I had seen while hypnotized. Finally, I knew I was becoming obsessed, and that if I couldn't put it out of my mind, then I needed to prove to myself beyond a doubt that I had made up everything from forgotten memories. As a police officer I had dealt with many people who were obsessed about something, and I knew that such obsessions often ended up hurting the people. So I decided that what I needed to do in order to get this matter out of my mind was to find undeniable proof that the things I had seen were simply patched-together memories from this life. I felt certain, if I planned my strategy properly, that doing this would only take a few hours.

As I sat down and developed my plan, it occurred to me that the portrait I had seen myself painting and the framed painting I had seen hanging over the fireplace in the mansion were probably famous, or at least semi-famous, paintings I had seen once in a history or art book. I had simply patched together a "memory of a past life" from subconscious memories of these events, which I had forgotten. So the obvious solution was to look for these paintings in an art or history book. Once I found the paintings and read about their history, I felt certain I would remember where I had seen them before. I took out a new yellow legal pad, started with "A" on the first page, and then wrote a different letter on each of the following pages. I knew I would need to keep an alphabetical listing of the books I had reviewed or else I would end up duplicating a lot of my effort.

And so, on my lunch hour for the next few weeks, this being pre-Internet days, I visited the Central Library in Indianapolis, which had an extensive collection of art books. The first day, when I began thumbing through the books of famous paintings and artists, I felt certain I would soon find one or both of the paintings. However, like most plans, this one didn't work out quite as conceived. I didn't find either painting right away, and I discovered that the library had hundreds of art books in its collection. Consequently, this work became tedious after the first few days, since I didn't have time to really study the paintings or read about them, only flip through the pages. I had to do it this way because if I didn't, I knew I would never get through the books, many of which contained hundreds of paintings. Still, I didn't really mind this tediousness because I felt confident of my ultimate success. A lot of really good police work has been accomplished this way. A lot of tough cases have been solved by a detective searching through ream after ream of information until the officer located the gem he or she was searching for.

I found, after several weeks of work and several hundred art books, that I had filled up the original legal pad and part of another. But I hadn't found either painting. When developing my plan, I had decided, to save time, to limit my search to only nineteenth-century painters. I couldn't be certain my subconscious mind hadn't simply made this fact up, but I reasoned I could expand my search later if necessary. I eventually came to the conclusion I needed to expand it because my search had obviously been too narrow, since I hadn't found anything. Yet, after several more weeks of tedious searching through the paintings of famous artists from the eighteenth, nineteenth, and early twentieth centuries, I still hadn't found either painting. Several times, my eyes had glanced at a painting as I flipped through the books, and I'd think it was one of them. I would stop, sparks filling my chest, but then after examining it more closely I'd find I was wrong. Still, I certainly wasn't ready to give up, because I knew I had to have seen the paintings somewhere. But more than that, I feared if I gave up now, my obsession would only worsen. I would never get the session with Dr. Griffith out of my mind. Unfortunately, I didn't know when I was conducting this search that I was wasting my time at the library, that I would instead have to travel almost a thousand miles in order to find one of the paintings.

CHAPTER FOUR

After another month and a half of the lunchtime searching, and an occasional day off spent at the library, this time looking through books of the lesser-known works of famous artists, I finally had to stop my investigation for a while and reconsider my original plan. It wasn't that I was tired of searching. I had never in my life been a quitter. As a matter of fact, I attribute a large part of my success as a student, as a police officer, and as a writer to just plain dogged determination. But even dogged determination won't serve you if it's aimed in the wrong direction.

So far, I had gone through every book in the library that contained photos of the well-known and even lesser-known works of famous artists and had filled up several legal pads, yet I'd had absolutely no success. Since I hadn't found either of the two paintings, I knew an error must exist somewhere in my original plan. For a while, I again considered the possibility that I could have just imagined both paintings, simply made them up in my mind. However, the clarity and the vividness of the paintings made that possibility very unlikely. No, they were real paintings. I was certain of it. But where had I seen them? To find out, I obviously needed a new plan and a new direction for my investigation.

After considerable thought, I finally decided to just let my search go idle for a time and give my subconscious mind time to come up with the proper resolution to the problem. This often works well in police investigations. An officer works on a case for a while and it seems to be at a dead end. And so he or she simply moves on to a new case and lets the old case sit. But the entire time he or she is working on the new case, the officer's subconscious mind is hard at work on the old case, and often the solution to the old case, or at least a new direction to take in the investigation, will come bubbling up to the surface.

For the next couple of weeks, even though engaged in the many demanding activities that come with being a police captain, I never really forgot about the two paintings. If I closed my eyes, I could still see them. And I still thought about my session with Dr. Griffith several times a day. But much more disturbing than any of this, I continued to dream about my session with Dr. Griffith. In one dream I found myself talking to an old man. I couldn't see his face, but I felt him to be wise and all-knowing. He told me that my stepdaughter and I had shared many lives before. In another dream, I was shown two books, again by the man whose face I couldn't see; one of the books was full of writing with no pictures and the other was full of pictures with no writing. The old man told me that these books showed the difference between my present and previous life. There was one dream, however, that I had at least a dozen times. In it, I saw myself and my older brother Fred as artists, sometimes at an artists' colony and sometimes in a studio together. All of these things made me aware that my obsession hadn't slackened much in the months since I had seen Dr. Griffith, and that I really needed to find a new direction, a new way of searching for the truth in this case. I needed to close out this episode and move on with my life. When the new direction finally did bubble up to the surface of my mind, it struck me as being so apparent and so obvious that I burst out laughing during the meeting I happened to be in when it occurred, which brought a table full of raised eyebrows since it was a budget meeting, hardly the forum for such a spontaneous outburst.

As we were discussing the figures for next year's expenditures, I suddenly realized that I had let my ego interfere with my investigation. I had assumed that any paintings my subconscious mind would tell me I had painted would have to be famous or at least semi-famous paintings, that they would have to be catalogued in books of great artists. More likely, I suddenly realized, the two paintings I saw during my session with Dr. Griffith were obscure, minor paintings by a minor artist. I had likely seen them once, and, for the very reason they were so minor, promptly forgot them. I simply needed to widen my search and go through books of lesser-known artists, and just forget about famous artists and masterpiece paintings. I also needed to expand my search beyond books and begin talking to people who might have seen the paintings or who could give me some useful information on how to find them.

When I initially began my search for the paintings, I had assumed that finding them would take only a few hours of work, but that I would certainly find them. The months of fruitless searching hadn't discouraged my belief that I would eventually find them; it only readjusted my estimate of the work that would be necessary. But this increased difficulty, I knew, would only make finding them that much more satisfying. When I arrived home that evening, I got out the Yellow Pages and a street map of Indianapolis and began circling all of the art stores and galleries in Indianapolis. My search, I realized, would be much easier if I could systematically visit these locations without a lot of doubling back.

Two months later, however, after reviewing every art book in the library's collection, and after visiting every art store and gallery in the city, hoping to find that one person who might have seen either of the two paintings, I again felt stymied, but certainly not ready to give up. If I gave up now, I knew I would always wonder if just a little more searching could have solved this case. However, I hadn't found anyone or anything that could verify the paintings even existed. Every art gallery told me the same thing—even if I knew the artist's name or the names of the paintings, locating them would still be extremely difficult because, in those pre-Internet days, there existed no central registry of paintings in the United States. Even if I knew the artist's name or the names of the paintings, I would still have to start calling every art dealer and gallery in the United States in order to find them. And with only a description of them, which was of course all I had, my search, art dealers assured me over and over, was almost certainly doomed. But regardless of this ominous forecast of failure, I refused to quit. Both of these paintings had been too vivid in my hypnotic regression not to be real. They had to be real paintings I had seen once and simply forgot about. I just knew it. They could be found. It would just require a lot of work.

This investigation, I had to continue to reassure myself after all the months of no success, was no different than investigating a crime where finding just one specific piece of evidence would solve it. I knew what this one piece of evidence was, and that with enough diligence it could be found. I just had to work harder. If I gave up, I would have to admit that I had failed in what should have been a relatively easy investigation, and I wasn't ready to do that. And so, I next began visiting the various bookstores around Indianapolis: B. Dalton, Walden's, Half Price Books, Borders. I did this because all of these stores, I found, carried art books the library didn't. I particularly liked going to Borders because not only did they have a huge collection of art books, they also had chairs and stools, which made the searching less tiring, though after visiting the store a few dozen times without purchasing anything, my presence began eliciting raised eyebrows from the staff every time I walked in. Yet still, even though I spent several months in bookstores, success continued to elude me.

I again found myself stymied, and finally began to get a bit discouraged about the possibility of success. Through all of my hundreds and hundreds of hours of searching, the only thing I had turned up were two paintings that resembled the one I had seen hanging over the fireplace in the mansion. In both cases, though originally excited, when I closed my eyes I could still see the colorful still-life painting in the mansion, but I could also see the differences between it and the two I had found in the art books. Also, I couldn't find any connection between myself and the paintings I had found in the books. I had no sudden snap of memory that said, "Oh yeah, that's where I saw it!"

Still, I refused to give up. My almost daily obsession with the regression hadn't slackened at all, nor had the dreams, and I feared the obsession wouldn't disappear until I had resolved this. In addition, finding the paintings had turned into a challenge of my investigative skills, a challenge I would meet and overcome. And so, similar to what a detective does when handling any other difficult case, I decided that I simply needed to change the direction of my investigation again.

The new direction I needed to take, however, didn't jump right out at me. After considerable thought, I finally decided that before any new direction could be decided upon I first needed more information. During the previous months of searching, the only information I'd had to go on was the vision of two paintings. Before I could decide on a new direction, what I needed was a little more information about the painter or the paintings.

I decided therefore to begin again at the source. And so, even though I hadn't yet gotten over the embarrassment of my first session, I visited Dr. Griffith for a second hypnotic session in the hope of recovering more information, in the hope that another trip back to the supposed artist's life would perhaps give me insight into where I had gotten the information about him. I told Dr. Griffith what I was attempting to do and how I wanted to try to obtain more information about the artist's life when I called to make the appointment. She didn't seem to have any problem with it and welcomed me back graciously when I appeared for our second session.

However, after the initial walk-through and imagery, and even after I found myself going into the same hypnotic state I had been in on my first visit, absolutely nothing happened when she tried to take me back to the artist's life. Then, on the possibility that one of my wives might have shared the artist's life with me, she tried to have me go back to a life I had shared with my first wife, and then with my second wife. But like the artist's life, nothing happened, no matter what approach she tried.

Finally, Dr. Griffith simply let my subconscious mind pick a life, and I soon found myself in the body of an Asian man around the time of the first millennium. I somehow knew I was a soldier who worked as a scout for a large army. In one scene, I found myself riding a horse through a small village and discovered that the inhabitants, upon seeing me, fled in terror. When Dr. Griffith asked me what I was doing, I said I was looking for gold. In another scene, I occupied the body of the scout as he stood on a large hill overlooking a huge walled city. As I looked down upon the city, I told her, "That's where the gold is."

Upon Dr. Griffith's instruction I fast-forwarded to a scene in which the army I was a part of had laid siege to the city. She then told me to fast-forward until I went into the city, but I told her, "I didn't get into the city." Instead I witnessed a scene in which an arrow fired by one of the city's defenders struck me in the throat and I died.

I next moved on to a life in which I found myself as a monk in Medieval Europe. I told Dr. Griffith that I had been sent by my superiors to a village, where my job was to attempt to educate the villagers. The inhabitants of the village, however, were more interested in getting enough to eat, which they seldom did, than they were in learning anything. At the scene of my death, I felt I had been a failure because I hadn't interested even a single person in learning anything. "The village was ignorant," I told Dr. Griffith. "They didn't want to learn anything. I couldn't teach them anything. I accomplished nothing."

Following this life, Dr. Griffith told me, "Go to a life when you could help people, when people would listen to you. Go to a life when you were a valued person."

I soon found myself in the body of a teacher in ancient Greece. It was a life in which I found myself revered in the city where I lived. In one scene, I found myself in a room full of students. They all listened intently to my words, as if everything I said should be written down and recorded.

At the completion of this life, Dr. Griffith made another attempt to get me to go to a life I had experienced with one of my wives. She tried several times in several variations, but again nothing happened.

After the session, I asked Dr. Griffith why I couldn't access the artist's life again. She simply shrugged and told me, "You apparently already know everything you need to know about that life."

While all of these new supposed past lives had certainly been interesting, they had been too far back in history to be authenticated, and they didn't help me at all in my quest to find out about the paintings or the artist. I knew I needed to try something else.

And so, when the second regression session didn't produce any results, I decided to try yet another approach. If I couldn't get more information on the artist or the paintings, then I needed to get more information on what might have happened to me while under hypnosis. With this information, I could perhaps understand why I had brought up the memories of the paintings. So, I began researching hypnotic-regression therapy, reading several dozen books and professional journals on the subject, both pro and con. I also found a New Age store in Indianapolis and visited it. Once inside the store, however, I felt a strengthening of my commitment to prove that my regression wasn't anything more than pieced-together forgotten memories. I knew I needed to do this because I simply couldn't make myself feel comfortable around the amulets, crystals, incense burners, and other trappings of the New Age. The store contained nothing that resonated with my life as a police captain. While there, however, I did purchase a dozen books about past lives and reincarnation, along with an audio tape that claimed it would teach me how to perform self-hypnosis and self-regression.

While reading these books during the next few weeks, I was surprised to find that many people who had undergone hypnotic past-life regression reported things similar to what I had experienced. After death, many people reported seeing themselves rising above their bodies, as I did. Most also saw themselves as being able to move through walls and ceilings, as I did, and many reported traveling around a bit before "going into the light," as I also did. The only difference in the accounts was that most of the people who reported that they stayed Earthbound and traveled about in the soul state, rather than going immediately into the light, said they did it because they wanted to check on the welfare of loved ones they were worried about. I had to smile. I figured I must be a really callous egomaniac since, in my supposed past life, rather than worrying about loved ones left behind, I imagined I wanted to take one last look at my paintings before I left Earth.

But more important than any of this, through all of the reading I stumbled onto another mystery. How could I have known these things happened when people in hypnotic regression saw themselves dying? How could I have known what happens after death? Had Dr. Griffith perhaps suggested them? I decided that had to be it. But after relistening to the tape of my session with her, I found she hadn't said or even suggested many of the things I had imagined myself doing. While she had instructed me to go up into the light, which would explain seeing myself floating, she hadn't said it before I first saw myself floating in the cave. And my flying over to see one of my paintings after I died had been completely contrary to her instructions to go up into the light. Then another thought occurred to me. I must have read about this. However, the only book I had read on the subject of past-life regression before visiting Dr. Griffith had been *Coming Back*, so I reread the book to see if the author had said anything about it. I found that *Coming Back* did make a reference to souls rising up out of the body after death and watching what happened. I figured my vision of passing through a ceiling and traveling long distances as a soul must have just been my own extrapolation of what I had read in *Coming Back*. After all, didn't all ghosts and spirits do that? But still, the realism of my regression experience made this explanation seem somehow weak. Being in the soul state had seemed very natural, not like something I had just imagined. Now I knew I really had to solve the mystery of where I had seen the paintings before and prove that past-life regression didn't exist, because the realism and clarity of what I had experienced always seemed to cloud any explanation I came up with.

Before I could do some parts of my research, I had to wait until an evening when both my wife and children were gone. I then locked myself in the den, turned off the telephone, and tried the self-hypnosis/regression tape. Actually, I tried it several times but could never come up with anything more than the vague impression of dense woods.

I had also read in several of the New Age books a number of scripts for self-hypnosis/regression that seemed to be very similar to Dr. Griffith's techniques, scripts that required a large amount of imagery. I tried this at least a dozen times, yet with absolutely no effect in all but two of these times. Those two times I did feel myself going into the same hypnotic state I had been in when I suddenly found myself in the valley I recognized. But both times the state lasted only a few seconds, and both times the only thing I sensed was the number 1917. Each time, the number came almost as an explosion that abruptly ended the hypnotic state.

Finally, after I finished the books and the tape, after months and months of investigation with no success at all, and after systematically reviewing and reconsidering everything I had done so far in the futile hope that I had overlooked something, I finally came to the conclusion that what I ought to do was just file this investigation away. I was out of leads and out of ideas. There comes a time when you finally have to quit, when you finally have to accept that you aren't going to be successful no matter how hard you work. In police work, there are often cases that just can't be solved. They have come to a dead end. What a police department does with these cases is simply file them away. They are not considered closed, just inactive. If at any time in the future new evidence should arise, then the investigation can be taken out, dusted off, and reopened. But until then, no real work is done on the case.

At this time, though, I didn't think that there was much of a chance this investigation would ever be reopened. I figured it would be one of those mysteries I would take to the grave. I could only hope that the passage of enough time would finally dampen and then eventually eliminate the obsession I was experiencing about the regression. I didn't realize that the new evidence I needed sat only two months and nearly a thousand miles away.

CHAPTER FIVE

Although I tried very hard during the next two months, I couldn't make myself forget about the session with Dr. Griffith, or even effectively decrease the frequency of thinking about it. Actually, on some days I found myself thinking about it even more than I had during the first few months after it occurred, occasionally a half dozen or more times a day. But even though the memories remained active in the forefront of my mind, I could never come up with anything new to do—with any new direction to take in the investigation—that would prove what I had experienced were just resurrected and re-ordered memories from my subconscious mind. So instead, I just told myself over and over that even though I apparently couldn't prove that what I had experienced were just dredged-up forgotten memories, I also had no proof they were anything else, and that for my own peace of mind I ought to just forget about the whole experience and get on with my life. This, however, had little effect.

Shortly after giving up the active investigation of my session with Dr. Griffith, Melanie began talking about taking a trip somewhere for our upcoming anniversary, somewhere neither of us had ever been. So, early one April morning she called me at my office.

"What do you think about going to New Orleans for our anniversary?" she asked.

It immediately sounded like a good idea to me. I had never been to New Orleans and had always heard it was a fun place to visit. I also had a friend there who I hadn't seen for a long time. But more important, I felt the distraction of a vacation was just what I needed to dampen the memories of my session with Dr. Griffith. I needed to have something to concentrate on other than the artist and the two paintings. "Sounds great to me," I told her. "I'll tell you what. Why don't we meet at the travel agency on our lunch hour?" After I hung up, I immediately began to feel better. For months I had longed to return to my life as it had been, with none of the supernatural trappings of the last few months. Maybe this would help.

"Late April is a fantastic time to visit New Orleans if you're not going for the Mardi Gras," the travel agent told us a few hours later. "Spring break's over and the weather's beautiful in April. Too early for the heat or mosquitoes."

We agreed, and when the travel agent checked, she was able to get us the flights we wanted, so we immediately booked two airline tickets. We also had the agent make reservations for five days at a first-class hotel in the heart of the French Quarter.

When our anniversary arrived, we flew down to New Orleans, picked up the rental car at the airport, and then drove to the hotel to check in. I found one thing about New Orleans our travel agent hadn't been correct about. She had been correct, of course, about the Mardi Gras being long over, and she had been correct about the weather being pleasant. But she hadn't been correct about spring break being over. The first evening Melanie and I ventured out into the French Quarter, we found it packed with partying college students. Every place we visited in the French Quarter showed evidence of the partying: from the piles of crumbled drink cups to the pungent odor of the inevitable pools of alcohol vomit. Hardly the ingredients for a romantic anniversary trip.

But regardless of the army of partying college students, we still found our first four days in New Orleans to be delightful. Melanie has always been a history buff, and we found (and she verified with her books and maps) that New Orleans and the surrounding area seemed to have something of historical significance at practically every stop. During our first four days, we visited countless antebellum homes, plantations, battlefields, and just about every site within a hundred miles of New Orleans that had any historical significance at all. New Orleans itself, Melanie lectured as she dragged me around the city from site to site, has a strong history it is proud of, from its days as a French settlement to its role in the War of 1812, and from its days as major port for frontier river traffic to its role in the Civil War. While we both enjoyed ourselves, more importantly, during the first four days I didn't think at all about my session with Dr. Griffith. The constant thoughts I had been having about the artist and the two paintings had been shuttled to the back of my mind.

On our second to last night there, we spent the evening with my friend Vicki, who I had met at a conference she and I attended in Vermont in 1985. After dinner, she drove Melanie and me around New Orleans and showed us some sights that are not on the usual tourist trails.

For our fifth and final day in New Orleans, I suggested to Melanie that we spend it window-shopping in the French Quarter. During our late-night forays to the various nightclubs in the French Quarter, I had noticed what appeared to be dozens of intriguing shops, art galleries, and antique stores that were always closed when we passed by them in the evening.

Once we started out on our window-shopping trip, I found I had been correct. We discovered the French Quarter to be host to dozens of interesting and unusual shops, art galleries, and antique stores. One of the first stores Melanie spotted turned out to be a large shop that sold historical memorabilia, and so, rather than just window-shopping, we spent a considerable amount of time inside. After this, we walked through a half dozen antique stores unlike any I had ever seen. In Indiana, if someone turns up an old rusty farm implement or tool while plowing, they brush it off and sell it as an antique. But the shops we visited in the French Quarter had fine old porcelain, beautiful nineteenth-century furniture, and even a brass Alvan

Clark refractor telescope. Being an astronomy enthusiast most of my life, I knew what a treasure a telescope like this was. But, of course, so did the antique store owner, who priced it as such.

On one of the streets in the French Quarter, Royal Street, we found several blocks of art galleries. The first few galleries we walked through turned out to be much larger than they appeared to be from the outside, often two or three stories. They were also exquisite in their art collections, with many fine pieces from the old masters. In one of the galleries, we stopped to admire a series of paintings that all seemed to have a similar theme and were obviously all painted by the same artist.

"They're scenes from a Wagner opera," a gallery employee commented when he saw us admiring them. "They used to hang in an Italian opera house."

In another gallery, we discovered a collection of paintings by such impressionist masters as Degas, Pissarro, and Manet. Although I have never cared much for Impressionism, Melanie does, so we spent some time in the gallery looking at them. Interestingly, even though we were looking at dozens of paintings, Melanie and I were having such a pleasant, relaxing time that the two paintings I had spent months searching for still rested quietly at the back of my mind.

I found, as we walked down the block, that the galleries seemed to become increasingly smaller, their paintings less expensive, and, of course, the artists much less well known. About two blocks down from the first gallery we had visited, Melanie and I stepped into a small art gallery. Melanie proceeded directly up a stairway just inside the door to look at a collection of modern art displayed on the open second floor while I began walking along the wall to my right, admiring the collection of paintings, but not recognizing any of the artwork or any of the artists. At the end of the wall, an easel stood in the corner holding a portrait. I gave it a glance and started on past, but then stopped abruptly, as if running into a glass wall. Whirling around, I stared open-mouthed at the portrait, reliving an experience I'd had once when I grabbed onto a live wire without knowing it, the current freezing me in my tracks as huge voltage surged up and down my arms and legs. Very similar to that experience, I simply stood frozen in the art gallery for what seemed like a long time, electricity racing up and down my arms as I stared at the portrait of the hunchbacked woman. This couldn't be, I told myself, feeling my arms now starting to shake as a dizziness seemed to fall over me like a net. It simply couldn't. What were the chances? What were the chances I could just walk into an obscure, little art gallery almost a thousand miles from home and find the portrait of the hunchbacked woman just sitting unpretentiously in a corner? Finally, I shook my head several times, trying to clear it. Even though I had spent months searching for this portrait, finding it was very much like walking in and unexpectedly finding my first wife dead: I didn't know what to do. At moments of truly intense shock, when unthinkable things occur, I have found that training and instinct really don't take over as you would expect. Instead, a person's mind seems to stumble blindly around searching for the correct response.

I had spent untold hundreds of hours searching through art books and questioning gallery owners in a quest for this portrait, yet I hadn't expected to find it like this, to just randomly stumble onto it, and I wasn't sure what to do. If I had found a picture of it in a book, I wouldn't have been surprised. Rather, it would have only confirmed my suspicion that the painting was famous enough to be included in a book of artwork, and consequently finding it in a book would have explained how I had seen it before, but had obviously just forgotten about it. Finding a picture of it in a book would have cleared up any hints of a supernatural explanation for my knowledge of it.

But I certainly wasn't prepared to find it like this. Not to just happen upon it by chance in an obscure little shop in a city I had never been in before. It was just too much of a coincidence, I told myself. Far too much of a coincidence.

A voice inside of me, a voice I recognized because it had been the voice that controlled my logical thinking all of these years, told me I had to be wrong about this being the portrait I had seen while hypnotized. What were the odds of just running into it like this? Far, far too large. I had to be mistaken. It just looked like the portrait was all.

But despite the voice of logic and reason, I knew I wasn't mistaken. This was the portrait I had seen while under hypnosis.

Closing my eyes as I stood motionless and still in shock in front of the portrait, electricity seeming to crackle off of my skin, I could once again see myself as the artist in the studio painting it, and I could once again see the hunchbacked woman, whose portrait I now stood in front of. I could see her posing in the studio, very erect, with stiff, raised shoulders. While it defied logical explanation, I was never more sure of anything in my life. This was the portrait I had seen myself painting.

Police officers don't like to encounter startling coincidences, such as the finding of this painting, because we so very often find that these events are actually staged events made to look like coincidences. Yet I didn't see how that could be the case in this situation. I kept closing my eyes and seeing the scene in the studio. What were the chances that I could just dream the scene up and then stumble onto a painting identical to the one in my imagination? Much, much too large, I decided. No, there had to be another explanation, a logical explanation. But at the moment no explanation came forward.

For the next several minutes, I didn't move from in front of the portrait, but instead continued closing my eyes to see again and again the scene of me painting this very portrait in my studio, and then opening my eyes to see the actual finished portrait. Every brushstroke was identical. The situation began to feel surreal, more like a very vivid dream that you wake up sweating from, a dream you have to keep telling yourself over and over was only a dream. It wasn't real.

Finally, however, even though I knew with absolute certainty that this was the same painting I had seen while under hypnosis, I convinced myself that stumbling onto it by accident like this was simply too bizarre to be true. I toyed with the idea for a few moments that perhaps I'd had some kind of stroke and just thought I stood in front of this portrait, when in actuality I was in a hospital bed somewhere or maybe even in a nursing home. After giving this possibility a few moments' consideration, I realized how very desperate I had become to find a rational answer for what was happening. But desperate or not, things like this just didn't happen in real life. What were the chances, I asked myself for the tenth time, that after all of the months of systematic searching, I would just happen upon the painting like this? What were the chances that Melanie would just happen to want to go to New Orleans, and that we would just happen to visit this art gallery just when they happened to have this painting for sale? No, it was simply too much of a coincidence to really be a coincidence. I had to be wrong about this being the painting. I just had to be!

For several moments, I tried to convince myself that the portrait just looked like the painting I had seen while under hypnosis, that was all. But as I kept telling myself this, I knew it wasn't true. This was the portrait I had seen myself painting. Absolutely no doubt about it.

Finally, once I reluctantly accepted the fact that this was the painting I had seen while under hypnosis, I realized the irony of the situation. During my thirty years as a police officer, I had always searched for the truth. Sometimes the truth didn't turn out to be what I expected, but still the truth was what I had always searched for. And now here I was, seemingly facing the truth I had been looking for, but at the same time trying to deny it, trying to find any way to deny the truth of what I had found. But I couldn't. This was undoubtedly the portrait I had seen myself painting while under hypnosis in Dr. Griffith's office. That was simply a fact, and I had to face it. What I needed to do now was just find a logical explanation for everything. This was not something supernatural, I insisted to myself. Supernatural things didn't happen to real people. Maybe they did in the movies, but not in real life. There had to be a logical, down-to-earth explanation, and I just had to find it. I began taking deep breaths, attempting to dampen the electricity that had now seemed to settle in my chest.

"I'll bet you're thinking how great that'd look over your fireplace, aren't you?"

The sudden voice crashed into my thoughts and startled me. I gave a little jump, and then turned to find a small, balding man in a dark suit smiling at me. I felt as if I had just been abruptly awakened from a deep, deep sleep. "Uh ... uh, yes, I was just admiring it," I said, trying to organize my thoughts. I immediately began looking for a signature on the painting. "Who's the painter? I don't think I recognize the work."

"Artist's name is Beckwith," the man said, walking over to an old wooden desk smothered under stacks of paper. "I think I've got a little bio on him." He searched through the stacks of paper on the desktop for a moment, then seemed to have a sudden thought and opened a long, deep drawer in the desk, and began thumbing through the files. "Ah yes, here it is." He pulled out a single sheet of white, 8½ by 11-inch paper, looked at it for a second, then walked back over and handed it to me.

"This piece is part of an estate we purchased," the gallery worker said. "I can let you have it very reasonably."

My stomach began filling with cold acid that seemed to bubble and froth when I saw the name of the artist, which was J. Carroll Beckwith. The name didn't mean anything to me, but the initial "J" did because I remembered telling Dr. Griffith that my name was Jack. But what really seized my eyes were the dates of his birth and death. Over and over I read "1852–1917." The acid in my stomach began to really churn as memories of the attempts at self-hypnosis rushed through my mind, particularly the two attempts that had ended abruptly with the single explosive thought: "1917." No, I told myself again, this was just too crazy. I was letting myself get carried away. There had to be some rational explanation that would eventually make me laugh at the possibilities I was considering.

Finally, forcing my eyes away from the dates, I read the single paragraph, the sloshing of the acid in my stomach making me feel queasy when I saw that Mr. Beckwith, born in Hannibal, Missouri, and living for most of his life in New York City, had studied in Paris under a painter named Duran. I had never heard of Duran, but I did remember telling Dr. Griffith that I thought I was in France. Beckwith, the bio also said, had won several prestigious awards for his paintings, including medals at the Paris, Atlanta, and Charleston exhibitions. I could suddenly see the scene in my regression in which people were congratulating me for some accomplishment.

Now, along with a churning stomach, I suddenly felt an attack of vertigo begin to seize me because I knew that at this very second my whole belief system was teetering and in danger of crashing down around me. I steadied myself. No, I insisted, this may look bizarre, but there still had to be some logical explanation. There had to be some way that I had known but forgotten about all of this information, something that would explain it all and then make me smile at its simplicity. And then suddenly, relief washed over me like a cool breeze when the explanation came to me.

"Has this painting ever been exhibited anywhere, in a museum maybe?" I asked. "I think I've seen it before. Or maybe it was in some kind of traveling exhibition or something."

I figured it was likely that I had seen this painting exhibited somewhere before, and along with seeing the painting I also saw some biographical information about Beckwith, but then just forgot that I had seen it. However, my subconscious mind, I felt certain, didn't forget it, and had probably used the information to invent the vision I'd had while under hypnosis. A tremendous feeling of relief seemed to suddenly make my body feel light and airy. I was positive this was the explanation, and that probably a similar explanation would explain most other past-life visions that people claimed were true. The difference was that most other people didn't look that hard for alternate, and more logical, explanations like I did. Because, if they had, they would probably have found one, just like I did.

"No," the man said, giving his head a slight shake, "you haven't seen this work before. This portrait's been in a private collection for years. And besides, let me be honest with you, I don't think there's been an exhibition of Beckwith's work in the last seventy-five years. He wasn't that famous. So, I can let this go very reasonably."

As the gallery worker's answer dashed my seemingly logical explanation for what had happened, the vertigo returned. My whole belief system was no longer just teetering. It was falling. Everything around me suddenly had such a surrealistic feeling to it that I could have been in a Kafka novel. And so I simply stood there open-mouthed, not knowing what to say, feeling numb and detached from reality. As I had discovered when my first wife passed away suddenly, when things that can't happen do happen, when the impossible becomes reality, your mind seems to detach itself from your body.

At this moment, Melanie came down from upstairs, and, after giving a quick look around at what hung downstairs and knowing I wasn't going to purchase anything, asked if I was ready to go. I had absolutely no idea what to do, and so I mumbled something to the gallery worker about wanting to think about the painting before I made any commitment, and then followed Melanie out.

The rest of the day, and our flight back to Indianapolis the next morning, all seem blurry and dreamlike to me now. I can remember visiting several more art galleries and antique stores, and I can remember eating that evening at a very nice restaurant on a large paddleboat moored across from Jackson Square in the French Quarter. But I really wasn't there. The shock of finding the portrait, and my desperate search for some logical explanation in light of what the gallery worker had told me, crowded out any thoughts of enjoying the remainder of our vacation. I kept asking myself: How could I have known that this specific painting existed if it hadn't been in a book or exhibited somewhere? How could I have seen the hunchbacked woman posing for me during the hypnosis if I hadn't seen the portrait somewhere before? The initial "J," the reference to France, the awards Beckwith won, and the date 1917 made me certain that all of this couldn't be just a coincidence. That would simply be too many right guesses for a coincidence. The gallery worker, I told myself over and over, had to be wrong. Yet, he had sounded like he knew what he was talking about.

But I also realized that the piece of evidence necessary to reopen the investigation I had closed two months ago had just shown up. I now had more than enough new information to conduct a thorough investigation. I knew exactly what I would do just as soon as I got back to Indianapolis. I would do a really thorough check on this J. Carroll Beckwith. When I did, I kept telling myself over and over, I would find the connection from where I had gotten my information about Beckwith. I would find it!

However, as I was telling myself this, I recalled my own often-given caveat: One of the worst things police officers can do is to become emotionally involved in their investigations. But I realized it was too late, much too late, to worry about that. In this investigation, not only was I emotionally involved, and had been for months, but I very, very desperately needed to solve this case and put it behind me. I wanted my life back. I wanted my life as a logical, rational person back. But to do this, I knew I had to rid myself of these supernatural trappings.

Chapter Six

Early on the first morning after arriving back home from New Orleans, in these pre-Internet days, I visited the Central Library again, but this time not just for a blind search of art books. I now had the information that could nail down the connection I knew existed, the connection that would logically explain where I had gotten the information about Mr. Beckwith and consequently put this whole episode behind me. I imagined that in a few months I would look back on the entire episode and smile at my own gullibility. Once I found the logical explanation I'd always known existed, I would likely laugh at some of the silly thoughts I'd had since finding the portrait.

I hadn't told Melanie anything about what I was doing, or why I was going to the library. She had already given me her opinion of my regression session—that it was all just my silly imagination. I didn't know if she had talked with detective Cathy Graban about my session, but if she had, she hadn't mentioned it to me. As a child-abuse detective, Melanie, of course, knew about many of the false accusations of childhood abuse that had come from regressive hypnosis, so she was very skeptical of it. And so, at this point I just didn't feel comfortable discussing with Melanie any of things I was thinking or doing. She had always been a very logical, facts-only person, and I knew she wouldn't be amused. Once I had disproved the whole past-life regression thing, I figured I would just keep everything I had done to myself.

By this time, I had published almost one hundred articles and short stories in national magazines, so I had become a fixture at the Central Library. I had conducted research there for more than fifteen years. Most of the librarians knew me, and I knew my way around the research resources. As a result, I knew exactly where and how to begin my research on J. Carroll Beckwith, and I expected to answer the questions I had and wrap up this episode in a fairly short time.

However, the first hour in the library quickly curbed my enthusiasm. I found that information on Beckwith required considerable searching, and what I located turned out to be scant at best. I discovered only four or five sentences about him in the large reference books on American painters, and none in many of the smaller reference books. I found it disquieting that the information available about Beckwith was so scarce because it shot holes in my theory that I had read his biography somewhere and then had just forgotten it. I did find one piece of information that gave me partial relief. The

"J" in J. Carroll Beckwith stood for James, not Jack. At that moment I didn't know how much this proved, but for some reason it gave me great comfort.

The little information I managed to dig up on Beckwith at the Central Library, with the exception of his first name, basically just confirmed the information I had already gotten in New Orleans. I didn't discover anything new or anything that disagreed with the information I already had. And so as a consequence, a single thought stood at center stage in my brain and shouted: If this is all the information available about Beckwith, where did I get the information I spewed out in Dr. Griffith's office?

The librarian who I eventually asked to assist me at the Central Library, after we had exhausted every resource they had, suggested that I try the library at the Indianapolis Museum of Art, since they had a much more comprehensive collection of art reference materials. That sounded like a good idea to me.

Leaving the Central Library in downtown Indianapolis, I drove straight up to the Indianapolis Museum of Art, a large limestone structure located on the city's north side. During the drive, I began having a minor attack of the same disorienting vertigo I'd had in New Orleans. The very lack of information about Beckwith was like discovering a lump in your side. It could mean nothing. But on the other hand, it could be extremely significant. Regardless, it was worrisome.

When I stopped by the information desk at the museum, the lady working there directed me to the second floor. After a rather long wait for the elevator, or perhaps only seeming long because I was in such a hurry, I finally stepped off onto the second floor and immediately walked into the library, which I discovered to be empty save for one other person and the librarians. Tiptoeing over to the counter, I asked one of the librarians if she could help me find all of the information they had on an artist named James Carroll Beckwith.

The young woman who assisted me turned out to be extraordinarily helpful. After a few minutes of searching, although she came back and said there were no books about Beckwith himself, she had still found several small mentions and references to him in a half dozen or so books about artists in general and one in a book about the American painter John Singer Sargent, who, I later found, had been a good friend and had shared a studio in Paris for several years with Beckwith. She also found a mention about Beckwith in a book on an artist named William M. Chase, with whom Beckwith had also apparently been a friend, and a short reference to Beckwith in an article about the early days of the Art Students' League in New York City, where Beckwith had apparently been an instructor.

"We've also got some information about an exhibition of Beckwith's work that was held here in Indianapolis," the librarian told me as she walked over to a file cabinet.

My heart jumped in my chest as my fist hit the table. I knew it! I knew it! The gallery worker in New Orleans had been wrong after all. There had been an exhibition of Beckwith's work, and it had been right here in Indianapolis. I had found the logical connection after all! I felt as relieved as if the doctor had just told me that the lump in my side was benign. A smile creased my lips when I thought about all of the silly ideas that had been going through my mind the last two days. This whole thing had a logical explanation after all. I had seen his work and had learned about him when his paintings were exhibited here in Indianapolis, but had just forgotten about it. Like most events that gullible people want to call supernatural, there was really a logical explanation after all. It just had to be dug out was all. The feeling of triumph was invigorating, the feeling of relief immense and sweet.

These feelings quickly turned sour, however, when I opened the manila folder the librarian handed me and found that the exhibition had been held in 1911. There was a yellowed newspaper clipping about the exhibition and an actual catalog from it, but that was all.

"Haven't there been any other exhibitions of his work since 1911?" I asked, hearing the tone of disappointment in my voice.

The librarian shook her head. "No, but the museum does have two of Mr. Beckwith's paintings in its collection." She picked up a sheet of paper and read from it. "Uh ... a portrait of a Mrs. William C. Bartlett and one of William M. Chase."

While my feelings of triumph over the exhibition had evaporated quickly enough, another earlier triumph also became short-lived. Upon reading several of the references about Beckwith that the art museum librarian had found for me, I discovered that Beckwith had always hated the name James and that during his youth he had invented and used other first names. He so hated the name James that for some years after he became an artist he had used only the initial "J," and in the last years of his life he dropped the "J" entirely and simply went by Carroll Beckwith. The reference didn't say what other names young Beckwith had used, but since I supposed Jack was a likely possibility as a substitute for James, the two initials matching, I had to drop this from a definite discrepancy to a weak one.

But no, I told myself, even if he had used the name Jack, that in itself wasn't disturbing, just an interesting coincidence, like him studying in Paris and dying in 1917. All just interesting coincidences. But my argument sounded weak, and the reference material I read next smashed into me like an unexpected wall in a dark room. Throughout his life, the reference said, Beckwith was known mostly as a portrait painter, even though he hated painting portraits. The reason for this, the reference book continued, was that portrait painting paid well, while other painting didn't, and so during his life, to survive financially, Beckwith had painted mostly portraits. I closed my eyes and brought back the scene during my hypnotic regression in which I had been in the studio painting the portrait of the hunchbacked woman. I remembered saying to Dr. Griffith, "I don't like doing portraits. But I need the money."

How could I have known that? How could I have known that Beckwith didn't like painting portraits but needed the money? Another coincidence? I didn't think so. As a police offi-cer, I've found that even though we are always highly skeptical of them, very rarely do startling coincidences occur during our investigations. However, they never come in bunches like this. Whenever more than one startling coincidence occurs, police officers say, "Whoa!" because we know that the things happen-ing are not coincidences. Something, or usually someone, is causing them to occur. But if all of this wasn't a coincidence, then what was it? What or who could be making this occur? My mind seemed to sputter at the implications of that ques-tion. Yet, like a man who finds his wife in bed with another man but tells himself that she still loves him, I kept telling myself there still had to be a logical connection somewhere. I just had to find it.

As I read on, though, instead of finding the logical answers I had hoped for, I instead began finding one disturbing fact after another that pointed in the other direction. One of the references to Beckwith that the librarian had found was a very short biography, actually not much more than a side note in a large book on American artists. The biography said that, when not doing portraits, Beckwith liked to paint plein-air studies of monuments, buildings, and landscapes; but, more important, that his paintings were full of sun and bright color. I remem-bered the painting I had seen through the window of the man-sion. It had contained a large sun and was full of bright color.

But most interesting of all was what I read in this short biography about Beckwith's death. He had died on October

24, 1917, in New York City. I immediately thought of the
scene during my hypnotic regression in which, after dying,
I rose above a huge city. I also recalled that it had appeared
to be a cold, blustery night, but not yet wintertime. It all fit.
There was no one startling and gigantic fact, just one small
confirmation after another. I had now given up thinking that
everything I was finding could be just one more coincidence.
Instead, I now felt totally confused and didn't know what to
think. The gears of my brain seemed to be turning slowly.

When I finished the half dozen references the librarian
had found for me, I realized it was actually a pitifully small
amount of information, probably not more than a page or
two if all put together. But more important, most of the
information I had found on Beckwith had been from this
library, and before this moment I had never been in an art
museum library. The amount available on Beckwith at the
Central Library, where I had of course been many times, had
been a third or less of this. The fact I had to face was that
there was just simply not that much information available
about Beckwith from sources I would have had contact with.

A desperate, brief attempt at one final logical explanation
flew through my mind but then crashed. I had never been
interested in American painters, and up until that day had
never heard of John Singer Sargent or William Chase, so I
knew I couldn't have known about Beckwith through reading about them. But even if I had read about them, which
I hadn't, the references to Beckwith in these sources were

pitifully small, and didn't contain much of the information that I seemed to know about him somehow. The truth was that I simply couldn't come up with an explanation for what I had found so far.

I began counting on my fingers and realized that, even with the pitifully small amount of information available about Beckwith, I had confirmed ten of the things I had seen while under hypnosis—and had disproved none of them. First off, I found the painting of the woman with the hunched shoulders. Then I confirmed that Beckwith had died in the fall, in 1917, and in a large city. I also confirmed that Beckwith had lived during the late 1800s and for a short time had lived in France. Additionally, I found that he had won awards for his paintings, that he was a portrait painter who didn't like painting portraits, but needed the money, and that he did paintings full of sun and bright colors. Again, nothing big by itself, nothing startling, but the way they added up told me that this was far too many coincidences to deal with. Far, far too many.

"Is this all the information you have on Beckwith?" I asked the librarian, hearing the near-pleading tone in my voice. "Aren't there any other books available somewhere, maybe books I could get locally or write away for that you don't have here?"

The librarian shook her head. "No, that's about the lot. Look, you've got to remember he died a long time ago, and he really wasn't that famous. I'm afraid there's just not that much interest in his life."

Regardless of what the librarian said, however, I knew there were two additional sources of information about Beckwith, sources I realized would either confirm everything else I had seen during my hypnotic session, or shoot holes in it, which I now desperately wanted to do. I so very badly wanted my old life back. I wanted this episode explained and behind me. However, I wasn't certain how easy these two additional sources of information would be to get.

I had found in the book on artist John Singer Sargent a notation that said the information concerning an anecdote about Sargent had come from a diary Beckwith had kept for most of his life, and which now sat stored in the archives of the National Academy of Design in New York City. Another short reference to Beckwith also said that at the last of his life he had written an autobiography, which, though never published, also now sat stored in the archives of the National Academy of Design in New York City. I knew that for my peace of mind I needed to somehow get a copy of Beckwith's diary and autobiography.

Thanking the librarian for her help, I left and took the elevator back downstairs, meaning to have a look at the Beckwith portraits they had displayed here. The woman at the counter, I discovered, who was just a volunteer, only knew where the general collections were hung, and had no listing of where individual paintings were displayed. Consequently, she had to call and let me speak with the museum's curator, who said that, yes, they did have two paintings by Beckwith. The portrait of William M. Chase, she said, was on display right then in the American Gallery, while the other portrait presently sat in storage. Thanking her, I hung up the telephone and asked the volunteer for directions to the American Gallery.

Once I entered the gallery, though, the first thing that attracted my attention was a large portrait, prominently displayed, of Indiana poet James Whitcomb Riley. It was an exceptionally well-done piece by an artist, I discovered on the metal plate below it, named John Singer Sargent. I found the coincidence interesting, but knew I was being distracted. I was looking for another painting. And though I had never seen the painting by Beckwith before, or knew what William M. Chase looked like, I knew instantly when I saw it which painting was Beckwith's. The reason I knew was because immediately upon seeing the large portrait I felt a huge surge of electricity running down and out my arms, and a return of the vertigo so strong that I became unsteady on my feet and had to get out of there.

A few minutes later, as I hurried out of the museum, I felt as though I had walked into another dimension. Nothing seemed to be as it had when I arrived there. It felt as if my whole world had been picked up, shaken, and then set back down. Everything was still there, but it all just didn't look right. I knew that I had to get my hands on those documents at the National Academy of Design as soon as possible. I still clung to the desperate hope that perhaps these documents would somehow explain the connection by which I knew what I did about Beckwith.

Unfortunately, they did.

CHAPTER SEVEN

I pulled out of the parking lot of the Indianapolis Museum of Art and immediately returned to the Central Library. Once there, I headed for the library's collection of telephone books, where I looked up the address of the National Academy of Design in New York City. As I scribbled down the address, I wondered what or how much I should say in my letter to them.

Later that afternoon at home, I sat down and composed the letter to the Academy, simply telling them that I was researching James Carroll Beckwith's life, which was true, and that I understood they had his diaries and unpublished auto-biography in their archives. I then inquired about how I could gain access to these documents. I suspected they would prob-ably tell me I had to come to New York City, but I hoped for an easier solution. While I certainly didn't relish the possibility of having to travel all the way to New York City, I knew I would if I had to. This case hadn't been out of my mind for almost a year, and I realized now that it wouldn't leave until I had some explanation for it. Once I finished the letter and put it in an envelope, I immediately drove down and dropped it in the mailbox, then told myself that there was nothing else I could do at this point, so there was no reason to ponder about possibilities or explanations until I received a response. With that, I resolved not to think about Beckwith or my session with Dr. Griffith until I heard from the National Academy of Design.

During the next week, however, despite my resolution, I thought of little else. As I waited for a response from New York, I felt disconnected from the world. Something had happened that defied rational explanation, and I found I had no resources to utilize that could make sense of it. Nothing I had ever learned or experienced in my life could be used as a reference. Somehow, and in some manner, I knew about the intimate details of a man's life that hadn't been recorded anywhere I'd ever had access to. Somehow I knew things about Beckwith that would only be easily explainable if he had been a famous painter such as Van Gogh or Rembrandt. A person, I reasoned, could easily come across intimate details about the lives of famous people such as these while reading, watching television, or at the movies. And while it would be easy to consciously forget knowing about these intimate details, the information would nevertheless be retained in the person's subconscious mind, ready to be pulled up in dreams or while under hypnosis.

With Beckwith, however, I couldn't use this explanation. He wasn't a famous or even a semi-famous painter. He had been simply a minor portrait painter who had lived and worked in New York City in the late nineteenth and early twentieth century. As far as I could find, he had never done anything or painted any canvas that would make him stand out from the thousands of other faceless and forgettable artists who had struggled to make a living by painting. As a result, the facts and details of his life, as with the lives of the other thousands of faceless artists, were not put down on paper or recorded anywhere readily accessible to the public. Proof of their existence would likely be noted only by a few obscure entries in public records that likely hadn't been looked at since they were recorded.

From the moment I discovered that Beckwith's diaries and unpublished autobiography existed, however, I realized that they would be the vital evidence that could decide what it was that had come bubbling up from my subconscious mind while I was hypnotized. In criminal cases there is often one crucial piece of evidence that can prove or disprove a case. Detectives naturally search for this definitive piece of evidence since it can close the case against the criminal. Beckwith's diaries or perhaps his autobiography would be the definitive piece of evidence that could close this case.

As I waited for the response from New York, finally giving up on the idea of not thinking about Beckwith, I knew that if I could just find a couple of the items I had spoken to Dr. Griffith about that could not possibly be true, then that would close the case for me. If I could find just two or three impossibilities, that would prove that the whole incident, though certainly bizarre and strange, didn't have a supernatural explanation. It wouldn't explain where I had gotten the ten facts about Beckwith that had proven correct, but the incorrect facts would show an inconsistency in the scenario that I had experienced while under hypnosis, and consequently make the entire incident likely just an incredible and bizarre series of coincidences, or maybe only a couple of amazing coincidences and a couple of lucky guesses.

After all, I told myself, beginning to feel as though perhaps I had a rational explanation after all, didn't a lot of artists probably visit France at some time in their lives? I didn't know, but it certainly sounded logical. And a fourth of all the people who died every year did so in the fall, and a hell of a lot of them died every year in large cities. It could be that some of the facts were just lucky guesses after all. Of course, even saying that half of the ten facts I had confirmed were just lucky guesses, that still left many more coincidences than I would be willing to accept in any police investigation. But if Beckwith's diaries or autobiography supplied proof that some of the other facts about his life were false, then that would be the only conclusion I could come to. I would have to believe that it was like winning the Powerball lottery jackpot, a one-in-a-hundred-and seventy-five-million chance, but something that does occur. Most important though, I knew I could live with that and then very happily put this incident behind me.

One morning, about a week and a half after mailing my letter to the National Academy of Design, I received a letter in the mail from them that said, yes, they did have possession of Beckwith's diaries and unpublished autobiography. They did not, however, the letter continued, lend these items out. As visions of me being forced to fly to New York City flittered through my head, I read the next paragraph, which said that the diaries and unpublished autobiography, however, had been microfilmed, and that I could obtain copies of this microfilm via interlibrary loan through the Archives of American Art at the Smithsonian Institute. And so, later that morning, I returned once more to the Central Library, this time filling out a request card for an interlibrary loan of the microfilm.

The next day, however, an employee of the library called to inform me that while the microfilm I had requested was available, the Smithsonian Institute had advised her that I could only have it for two weeks. I told her that would be fine.

Now that I had the microfilm coming, I knew I needed to make a list of what I would be looking for—things I could prove or disprove. I took out the audiotape of my session with Dr. Griffith, and, with paper and pen in hand, listened to it again. I jotted down everything I had said during the session that the diaries or autobiography could definitely prove or disprove, such as places, people, events, causes of death, etc. When I finished, I found I had twenty-eight items, twenty-seven from the session with Dr. Griffith and one from my own attempt at self-hypnosis, that could be proved or disproved by what Beckwith had written in his diaries or autobiography:

1. Did he paint the portrait of a
   woman with a hunchback?

2. Was the number 1917 important in his life?

3. Did he die in the fall of the year?

4. Did he die in a large city?

5. Did he live during the nineteenth century?

6. Did he and his wife spend some time in France?

7. Did he win awards or receive recognition for
   some of his paintings? Was he ever at a celebration
   where many people were congratulating him?

8. Did he paint portraits but hate doing it?

9. Did he paint portraits because he needed the money?

10. Were his paintings full of sun and bright colors?

11. Did he use the name Jack?

12. Did he use a walking stick?

13. Did he drink wine?

14. Did he express an almost desperate need for money?

15. In my regression, I saw myself arguing with someone
    about the poor lighting for one of my paintings.
    Can I find an incident of Beckwith doing this?

16. If Beckwith was married, did his wife's
    name sound something like Amanda?

17. Did Beckwith and his wife argue about money?

18. Did his wife play the piano?

19. Did Beckwith and his wife have children?

20. I said during the regression that my wife could not have children. Could Beckwith's?

21. In my regression, I said my wife and I were happy, even though we didn't have children. Were the Beckwiths happy?

22. In the regression, I saw myself working in a studio with lots of windows and skylights. Did Beckwith?

23. Did Beckwith ever visit or stay at an estate with a large garden?

24. Did a woman very important to Beckwith die of a blood clot?

25. I described my studio as being filled with unsold paintings. Was Beckwith's?

26. I said, "I'm a good painter, but it took so long." Did Beckwith feel at the last of his life that he was finally successful or a good painter?

27. I said during the regression, "I'm happy when I paint." Was Beckwith?

28. In my regression, I said, "I don't think they liked me, but they liked my paintings." Was this true?

The fact that I had already at least partly confirmed the first ten of these twenty-eight items made me that much more anxious to get my hands on the microfilm and get this over with. I had found during the last year that there is nothing worse than the anxiety of uncertainty. It was like living with a spouse you suspect is being unfaithful. The uncertainty turns out to be worse than the infidelity. If you could only be sure one way or the other, you could deal with it. Not knowing, though, leaves you in a situation where you don't know what to do. You are simply floating in a state of constant anxiety, the uncertainty gnawing at your insides like an unknown cancer. I truly and desperately longed to get this event behind me. Before my session with Dr. Griffith, my life had been solid and structured. I had dealt only with things that could be seen, sensed, and proven. Before the session, I had never concerned myself with or had any belief in otherworldly things, in supernatural explanations. That was for television programs like *The X-Files*. I wanted my old life back.

I needed closure, and I knew that the diaries and unpublished autobiography were the only things that could do that.

When about a week later the library employee finally called and said that the microfilm had arrived, I immediately drove to the Central Library. Fortunately, I had been doing research at the Central Library for most of my married life. In the preceding ten years, I'd had a large number of articles published, some in big magazines such as *Reader's Digest* and the *National Enquirer,* but many more in police-management

magazines, and had done much of the research for these articles at the Central Library. This meant I didn't have to explain
to my wife why I was spending so much time there. Actually, I
hadn't told her anything about what I was doing, other than
what I had told her about my first visit to Dr. Griffith. I felt
certain she didn't have a clue as to what I was researching,
and probably thought that I had forgotten all about my session with Dr. Griffith. Several times in the last year I had considered telling Melanie what I was up to because I valued her
advice, but after a little thought, I didn't believe it would be
a good idea at this point in the investigation to let her know
what I was looking into. While Melanie was usually supportive, I really didn't think she would be in this case. Rather, I
worried she would think that the explanation for everything
was that my mind had slipped a few gears, so I decided I
wouldn't tell her anything until I had this case nailed down
one way or the other—and maybe not even then if I could
prove the regression wrong.

When I appeared at the interlibrary loan desk and told
the person there who I was and what I wanted, the attendant
had me fill out a card for the microfilm and then asked for
my library card, which, she said, would be returned when I
returned the microfilm (one of the conditions of the loan
was that the microfilm had to stay in the library). She then
handed me a box that was about a foot square and directed
me to the microfilm room.

A few minutes later, I sat down at one of the microfilm machines and opened the box, finding that it contained nine spools of microfilm. I didn't know how much information was on each spool, but after I loaded the first spool into the machine and looked at the table of contents, I received a sudden and very sobering glimpse into the magnitude of the task I had undertaken. Beckwith had kept a daily diary from age nineteen up to the day before he died at age sixty-five. I sampled a number of pages from several spools, and found that he had used diaries that allotted a page per day. A little quick mathematics in my head told me that the diaries, along with one microfilm spool of photographs Beckwith had taken during his life and Beckwith's unpublished autobiography, added up to well over 17,000 frames of microfilm. I then quickly estimated that if I took only thirty seconds to read each page, it would still take me, working three hours a day for two or three days a week (which was all my schedule would allow considering I had a family and a full-time job), at least a couple of months to review the spools, to say nothing of the time necessary to take notes or make copies of pertinent pages.

Since I only had the microfilm for two weeks, I knew I needed to make some kind of decision about what I was going to do. I finally decided that I would read the autobiography, and then, if necessary, sample one year each from four or five of the spools. All I really needed was just to be able to show that two or three of the things I had seen while under hypnosis were impossible. For example, I had said while under hypnosis that my wife and I had no children. So, if the Beckwiths turned out to have children, then that was that. Or if Beckwith turned out to be a teetotaler, then my seeing him drinking wine at the outdoor restaurant would also have been impossible. I could then close this case and just remember the episode as being one of the most amazing strings of lucky guesses and coincidences a person could likely experience. It'd be no more improbable than a gambler winning some huge long shot, and people did that all of the time. If I could just find this evidence, then I could close this case and go back to my nice, structured, orderly life.

CHAPTER EIGHT

As I loaded the microfilm containing Beckwith's autobiography into the machine, my hands began tingling with anticipation. From the very small amount of material I had been able to uncover so far about Beckwith, I had already made a surprising number of confirmations of what I had seen during my hypnotic regression. However, I knew that what I was about to read would either prove that I had only experienced an incredible string of lucky guesses and coincidences or change my view of the world forever. I took a deep breath and brought the first frame into focus.

On September 23, 1852, in the small village of Hannibal, Missouri (the boyhood home of Mark Twain), Martha Melissa Beckwith gave birth to a nine-pound baby boy. The father of the newborn, Charles Henry Beckwith, had been out shooting that morning with a Mr. Carroll, a native of Ireland on an extended tour of America. As a consequence of this, the

Beckwiths named their new son James Carroll Beckwith. There was no mention of how the Beckwiths decided on the child's first name, but James Carroll Beckwith reportedly disliked the name James intensely. In later life, he would sign his name J. Carroll Beckwith, and then eventually drop the "J" altogether. His death certificate and the headstone on his grave, I was to find later, identified him as simply Carroll Beckwith.

Carroll's father, a surveyor by trade, had come to live in Missouri because he had heard and believed that a man of his talents and training could prosper greatly in what was then considered wilderness territory. This had seemed logical to him since settlers in these largely uncharted regions would naturally need their newly claimed properties surveyed. Charles Beckwith, therefore, in a quest for prosperity, quit a teaching position he held, packed up his family, and moved them from Oxford, New York, to Hannibal, Missouri.

The Beckwith family, however, didn't find the happiness they expected, nor the promised prosperity, because the 1850s in Missouri were anxious years of ever-heightening tensions due to the slavery question and the events leading up to the Civil War. Charles Beckwith, while personally opposed to slavery and not owning any slaves himself, did nevertheless lease some of them from neighbors. In his autobiography, which he titled *Souvenirs and Reminiscences—A Book of Remembrance*, Carroll Beckwith tells about having a "Negro Mammie" while the family lived in Missouri.

Charles Beckwith, not willing to give up, and still believing he could find prosperity, decided to move his family from

Hannibal, Missouri, to Chicago, Illinois, when Carroll was still a very young child. At first, the living conditions of their new home in Illinois didn't far surpass the old life they'd led in Missouri. Chicago in the 1850s was a rugged town still in its infancy. In his autobiography, Carroll recounts a story his mother told him of how some workmen posted a sign next to a mud hole in the street that warned passersby the hole had no bottom.

Eventually, however, unlike in Missouri, Charles Beckwith did prosper in Chicago, founding the C. H. Beckwith Wholesale Grocery business at South Water and Dearborn Streets. His wife, though, despite their increasing affluence, longed to return to the refinement of New York, and she and her children, including Carroll, often spent their summers at the family farm in Oxford, New York. Charles Beckwith, however, continuing to succeed very well in the wholesale grocery business, refused to yield to his wife's entreaties to leave Chicago.

When the Civil War broke out in 1861, Carroll was only nine years old, too young to have to worry about being called up for military service. Still, a strong sense of the need for preparedness swept the country, causing military schools to begin springing up everywhere. This change in the country's attitude about preparedness also brought about a change in the Beckwith household. Charles Beckwith, a strict disciplinarian who had always felt that his wife was much too soft with their three sons, enrolled Carroll and his two brothers, Frank and Charley, at the Starr Military Academy in Yonkers, New York.

Carroll, however, didn't remain enrolled there very long. A severe attack of rheumatism, an affliction that would haunt him for many years, forced the family to remove Carroll from the school and bring him home, where they placed him under the instruction of a private tutor. Charles, however, still felt that Carroll needed the discipline of a military academy, and, once Carroll had recovered from the rheumatism, Charles enrolled him in yet another military academy. The rheumatism, however, returned with such ferocity that his parents sent Carroll, who was now confined to a wheelchair, to a water cure in the hope of relieving the severe pain. (In the 1800s, many believed mineral-water baths and the like had therapeutic effects.)

After Carroll had recovered sufficiently enough that he no longer needed a wheelchair, his father, not easily discouraged, enrolled him in yet another school, this one in Painesville, Ohio. Carroll, however, now sixteen and not liking the rigid atmosphere of the school, decided to leave. Late one night, without telling anyone, he packed his trunk, took the omnibus to the train station, and caught a train back to Chicago. When he walked into the Beckwith home at 140 Michigan Avenue, his father, sitting at the breakfast table, looked over his paper at him, but made no comment.

Because of Carroll's poor health due to the constant bouts of rheumatism, which became so bad in 1869 that his family sent him to New Orleans to recover, not only did Carroll's father finally give up on the idea of sending him to a military school, he also did not insist that Carroll work at the family business, as did his two brothers. Instead, Carroll, with his mother's assistance, persuaded his father to allow him to attend the Chicago Academy of Design, where he received his first training in art. Carroll's father, though, while reluctantly allowing his son to attend art classes, still believed, and often stated, that being an artist was the best way he knew of starving. He didn't encourage Carroll's career choice in any way. Carroll's mother, though, being much more supportive, bought him his first easel, brushes, and paints for Christmas. Carroll quickly immersed himself in his art and, despite his father's resistance, dreamed of a career as a professional artist.

This standoff between Carroll's artistic career aspirations and his father's expectations continued until October 9, 1871, when a catastrophe swept through Chicago, destroying the Beckwith home and family business. While this catastrophe would thrust the Beckwith family into serious financial difficulties, it would at the same time propel Carroll into his career as an artist. The summer of 1871 had been both exceedingly hot and dry. This made Chicago, with its streets paved with tar-soaked logs, its sidewalks constructed of wood, and many of its buildings made of lumber, a tinderbox waiting to ignite. On October 9, 1871, it did ignite and a fire of huge proportions, beginning on the west side and quickly spreading, burned down everything in its path. At 10:00 a.m., October 10, 1871, the fire reached and burned down the Beckwith home on Michigan Avenue. The C. H. Beckwith Wholesale Grocery business on Dearborn Street had already burned to the ground, leaving absolutely nothing behind. Charles Beckwith, while having time to remove a considerable amount of cash from his business before it burned, unwisely stored this money in his home, and then lost it when his house burned down.

The resulting devastation of the fire, leaving no family business or home, finally extinguished his father's opposition to Carroll wanting to become an artist. Charles arranged for his son to live with an uncle in New York City and study art there. The uncle, John H. Sherwood, had earlier made a fortune speculating in real estate, and owned a home on Fifth Avenue. On October 31, 1871, Carroll packed his clothes and prepared to leave Chicago for New York City.

Once situated in New York City, Carroll enrolled at the National Academy of Design. However, because of a severe attack of rheumatism in April 1872, Carroll's father traveled by train to New York City and brought Carroll back to the family's new home in Morgan Park, Illinois, a suburb of Chicago, where Charles Beckwith now speculated in real estate. In November 1872, having recovered sufficiently from the rheumatism to return to New York City, Carroll reentered the National Academy of Design.

Eventually, however, even though staying in relatively good health for the next year and receiving excellent art instruction in New York City, Carroll decided that to truly prepare himself for his life as an artist, he needed to study in France. A number of his former classmates at the National Academy of Design had already moved to France and enrolled in art schools there.

Although aware of his family's perilous financial situation, Carroll persuaded his father to support him while he studied in France.

On October 13, 1873, Carroll sailed from New York City, bound for England on the S.S. *Italy*. The ship, actually little more than a freighter, which Carroll had booked himself on because of the cheap passage, took seventeen days to finally reach Liverpool, England. Carroll stayed in England for a little over two weeks, but found the climate atrocious, and on November 18, 1873, he sailed for Calais.

Upon finally arriving in Paris, Carroll immediately went to Picot's restaurant, where, according to letters from former students of the National Academy of Design, the American art students in Paris always congregated. At the restaurant, he indeed found several of the men he had studied with in New York City. Although glad to see him, they told Carroll he had arrived at a bad time, that the situation in Paris had changed, and he would have extreme difficulty getting himself accepted by any good art school.

Indeed, upon making the rounds of the art schools, Carroll found that these institutions were not open to new students. One of the reasons for this, he discovered, was because so many French students had enrolled in them. Students accepted by one of these schools received a deferment from military service. Finally, though, a friend mentioned to him that a new art school had been opened by the recently acclaimed painter Carolus-Duran (real name: Charles Durand). Carroll took samples of his work to this school and gained admittance.

Another young American art student, John Singer Sargent, also enrolled to study under Carolus-Duran at the same time. Soon, Carroll and Sargent had both progressed so well in their art training that Carolus-Duran asked them to assist him when he was engaged to paint a large ceiling decoration at the Louvre. In this rendering of *The Glory of Marie de Medicis*, the three men used their own faces on some of the subjects.

Despite his progress under Carolus-Duran, in the fall of 1874, Carroll applied to study at the Ecole des Beaux-Arts. Although the school didn't accept Carroll that fall, it did accept both him and Sargent in the spring of 1875. As fellow students, Carroll Beckwith and John Singer Sargent took rooms together at No. 73 rue Notre Dame des Champs in Paris. They would live together for the next several years and become lifelong friends, even though Sargent's fame would far eclipse Carroll's, as would his earnings from painting.

When I was randomly looking through Beckwith's diaries to ascertain how much information the nine spools contained, I happened onto a diary entry dated June 16, 1875, which caught my attention because for some reason it had been excerpted and typed. The entry told about how during the summer of 1875, while school at the Ecole des Beaux-Arts stood in recess, Carroll had toured Italy and Germany, studying the art of both countries. He recounted that while staying in Venice he regularly visited a restaurant where he dined on burned eggs and wine.

Once he had completed his art education at the schools in Paris, Carroll traveled around Europe for some time before finally returning home to Chicago in 1878. However, after spending the last seven years in New York City and various large cities in Europe, the frontier quality of Chicago seemed suffocating to him. In 1879, Carroll moved to New York City, where he and painter William Merritt Chase, who would eventually become almost as famous a painter as Sargent, established the painting and drawing departments of the newly formed Art Students' League, where Carroll would be an instructor for eighteen years. The Art Students' League was a student-run and supported institution, located over Hearn's store on 14th Street in New York City. Being an unendowed institution, the League's fees were higher than traditional schools, but nevertheless large numbers of students flocked there, attracted both by the freedom allowed and the excellent instruction.

A female artist who attended the Art Students' League in the 1880s wrote an article about her experiences while a student at this school, which appeared in the January 1987 issue of the *Archives of American Art Journal* (though the author had died over forty years earlier). In the article, the author states that, though she never took a class from Carroll Beckwith, the other students felt him to be an excellent instructor, and one of the most popular there.

In 1879, Carroll Beckwith, near the beginning of his career as an artist, received considerable recognition and acclaim among the painters in New York. His portrait of Mrs. R. H.

McCready, though painted when he was only twenty-five, was shown in an exposition and received high praise from the critics. The painting became known as *The Lady in Red*. Even though throughout his life his artwork would never receive the recognition or demand the price that John Singer Sargent's would, Carroll Beckwith's painting did receive recognition, including medals at art expositions in Paris, Atlanta, and Charleston.

On June 1, 1887, Carroll Beckwith married Bertha Hall, the daughter of a prominent New York merchant. They remained married until Carroll's death in 1917. The Beckwiths lived for most of their married life in New York City, and alternated spending their summers in Europe or at their summer home in the mountain village of Onteora in the Catskills, where Carroll had a studio and taught art classes. Carroll and Bertha Beckwith had no children.

In 1910, Carroll closed up his studio in New York City and announced that he planned to move to Italy. There he hoped to be able to live cheaper, make more money, and perhaps work on something other than portraits, which was what he had been mostly painting since moving to New York City in 1879. A short biography of Carroll Beckwith in *American Art Analog* stated: "In all probability, said one of his colleagues, mural painting would have brought out Beckwith's best powers, but portraiture paid the most during his lifetime, so he painted portraits."[1]

---

1   Michael David Zellman, *American Art Analog*
     (New York: Chelsea House Publishers, 1986), p. 481.

However, finding himself no more successful as an artist and disliking the weather in Italy, Carroll Beckwith eventually returned to the United States. In October 1911, the John Herron Art Institute in Indianapolis held an exhibition of Beckwith's work, while in April 1912, another exhibition of his paintings opened in Chicago. At around 5:00 p.m., October 24, 1917, after returning from a walk in Central Park, Carroll Beckwith collapsed in the lobby of the Schuyler Hotel on West 45th Street in New York City, where he and Bertha lived. Several people carried him to his suite and summoned a doctor, but he died soon afterward. The following spring, Bertha auctioned off 188 of Carroll's paintings through the American Art Galleries at Madison Square South in New York City. A booklet from this sale said: "In his paintings of Versailles, Mr. Beckwith has naturalized the art of the French among us. He is most admirable in his rendering of those gardens and their exquisite details. In them he reveals a range of expression surprising to those who think of him as a portraitist solely."

If the above biography of Carroll Beckwith seems much fuller for the first twenty-one years of his life than for the remaining forty-four, that is because age twenty-one was as far as he got in his autobiography. Begun in the last year of his life, in the spring of 1917, when Carroll and Bertha resided in Santa Barbara, California, his autobiography spans only twenty-three typed pages. The remaining history of his life I gleaned from various obscure art reference sources I found when I returned to the bookstores I had haunted while hunting for the two paintings, most of the sources seldom containing more than a paragraph or two on Carroll Beckwith, if he was even mentioned at all. More often than not, he wasn't.

Still, even these sparse mentions had to be double-checked for accuracy since they occasionally disagreed on the facts of his life. For example, in *Who Was Who in American Art*, the authors list Carroll Beckwith's death as a suicide, while he actually died of a heart attack. As a part of my research, I obtained a copy of his death certificate from the New York City Archives, which states he died of chronic endocarditis. This is an infection of the heart valves, and it was usually fatal in the early 1900s. However, to be certain the claim of suicide in *Who Was Who in American Art* was an error, I called Dr. Jeffrey Burkes, medical examiner, in New York City. I asked Dr. Burkes if he would check the records from 1917 and verify what Carroll Beckwith had died of. Dr. Burkes called me back the next day and said that Carroll Beckwith had definitely died of a heart attack.

Of course, verifying facts wasn't my largest problem after reading Beckwith's autobiography and the other sources. The largest problem by far was that in this short reading I found four new confirmations of what I had seen while hypnotized. Each time I would come across another confirmation, it felt as though my stomach squeezed just a little tighter, until at the end it seemed to be the size of a walnut. And just as important, or maybe even more so, I found absolutely nothing that disproved anything I had seen while under hypnosis.

I pulled out the written list of questions I would be trying to answer while reading Beckwith's autobiography and the other sources. From this short reading, I checked off that I found confirmation of question 19. During the regression, I told Dr. Griffith that my wife and I had no children, which the Beckwiths didn't. I also discovered that I had answered question 23. Beckwith had painted the gardens at Versailles, which could very easily have been the large garden I saw myself in while hypnotized. For question 16, though I found that Beckwith's wife's name was Bertha, which does sound more like Amanda than does Joyce, Mary, Helen, or any one of thousands of other female names, this certainly wasn't close enough for me to consider it a confirmation. However, this lack of confirmation didn't surprise me because during the regression, when Dr. Griffith had asked me for the name of the woman I was walking to meet on the city street, I had felt myself reaching, and hadn't felt confident at the time that Amanda was correct. Interestingly though, and as I will talk about in a later chapter, several years after the first edition of this book an independent researcher turned up information that shows where the name Amanda likely came from.

I also found that I had confirmed question 13 when, upon randomly glancing through Beckwith's diary to ascertain how much information it contained, I found that Carroll Beckwith did drink wine, which I saw him do at the sidewalk cafe during my hypnotic regression. Lastly, I found that Carroll and Bertha had made many summer trips to Europe. In my regression I saw them together in France. This, I felt, however, was only half a confirmation because, while I was certain they probably visited France often during their summers in Europe, since Carroll had lived and studied there for five years, I didn't find this fact specifically mentioned. Also, in the reading I found no dates for when he had painted the gardens of Versailles (which, of course, are in France), so I didn't know if this had been before or after his marriage.

In addition to these new confirmations, several of the short biographies I found at the bookstores gave additional confirmation to some of the things that I had earlier discovered. For example, they too said that Beckwith only painted portraits because they paid the most and he needed the money, something I said while in Dr. Griffith's office. And I found more information about how Carroll Beckwith, though never financially successful, had won some prestigious awards for his painting, which fit well with the scene I saw while hypnotized, in which everyone present was congratulating me for some achievement.

Once I finished Beckwith's autobiography and the other sources I had found, I asked myself: Now what am I going to do? But before I had even finished posing the question, I already knew the answer. I really had no choice. I had to read the entire collection of Carroll Beckwith's diaries. I had to read and analyze the entire nine spools of microfilm. I knew I could no longer rationalize that this was all just some string of amazing coincidences, a series of lucky guesses, or that it could still be explained by my lifelong belief system. The number of confirmations had grown much too large. Instead, feeling like a man who had lived his entire life in darkness and was suddenly seeing his first sunrise, I realized that I had apparently stumbled onto some type of universal truth.

However, I didn't feel the exhilaration I should have felt. After reading the autobiography and various short references, I felt similar to the way I had felt in the weeks following my first wife's unexpected death. I found myself suddenly living in a world that wasn't supposed to be. Something had happened that my life's experiences told me shouldn't have happened. Yet it did. I once again felt as if the thread holding my life to this world had snapped, and I was suddenly adrift, tumbling in a world where normal parameters meant nothing, in a world where I would have to learn how to function under a completely new set of rules.

And if I could verify as much as I had from just the small amount of information I had read so far, I almost feared what reading the thousands of pages of Beckwith's diary would bring. I strongly suspected that I wasn't going to find the "denying facts" I had earlier hoped for—the facts that would show me what I had seen while under hypnosis couldn't have really happened. If I was going to find this, I knew it would have shown up already. Still, I had more than a dozen facts left on my list that I would have to try to confirm before I could convince anyone else of what I had found. Actually, for most people I knew, trying wouldn't be enough. I would have to confirm *every* fact.

However, before I could begin with Carroll Beckwith's first diary entry on September 10, 1871, another concern immediately arose. Reading these thousands of pages was going to be tremendously time consuming, and I would be spending an awful lot of time at the library. I had already checked and found that I could extend the time allotted to me for the microfilm, and that, even when returned, I could request the microfilm again as many times as I wanted. However, I knew that eventually Melanie would want to know what I was researching so intently at the library, and why I hadn't produced any articles from it. While Melanie had always been a supportive, loving wife, I couldn't be sure what her reaction would be to the things I had found. Yet still, I felt it was time to tell her.

CHAPTER NINE

"Are you nuts? Have you lost your mind?"

This wasn't quite the reaction I had expected from Melanie, and for a moment I wasn't sure how to respond. Maybe I hadn't explained it properly.

While I was considering how else to tell her what I had found, Melanie looked at me with an expression that seemed to say she hoped this was just a lame attempt at a joke. "Come on, Bob, you don't really mean this. Tell me you're not serious."

I knew I probably shouldn't have been surprised at Melanie's reaction. She had always been a very grounded, down-to-earth, facts-only person. I realized that I needed to approach this from her strong points and let her see the all of information I had gathered.

I held my hand up in a stop signal. "Now hold on. You haven't seen any of my evidence. I know this all sounds a little crazy, but I can't come up with any other explanation for it."

Melanie now gazed at me as though wondering if perhaps I had suffered some kind of stroke. I realized I would never be able to convince her with just words. "I'll tell you what," I told her, "you listen to the tape and look at the evidence. Then, if you still think I'm wrong, give me another explanation. If you can come up with any other explanation that fits all the facts, I'll say I'm an idiot and shut up about it."

At the moment, I didn't feel frustrated or disappointed in Melanie's reaction, more just anxious. I wanted to see what her reaction would be once she had reviewed all the evidence. I wanted to see how her stick-to-the-facts-only personality dealt with it. And so, I gathered up everything I had collected so far, including hard copies of the relevant parts of Beckwith's autobiography and diary, and gave it to her.

Although Melanie had never been a devoutly religious person, I could see that once she realized I was serious, and thought about what I had told her, it went completely against the grain of her beliefs. She didn't want anything to do with such foolishness. Still, though, I kept insisting, and while at first refusing and insisting it was nuts, she finally agreed to listen to my tape and review the evidence. When she had finished, I waited for her response, but, uncharacteristically, she didn't have one right away. Instead, she seemed to be struggling with her answer.

"Well come on," I said. "If you think I'm nuts, what's your explanation?"

"I don't think you're nuts," she answered. "You're just mistaken is all. I think you probably picked up all of this stuff in a book somewhere, or you saw it in a movie or something." She shrugged her shoulders. "That's all there is to it. There's nothing special about it. You just forgot where you saw all that stuff you said."

"I couldn't have picked up the information that way," I countered. "There's no books about Beckwith. And there's sure as hell no movies about him. Don't you understand? Nobody cared about his life. Why would they? He wasn't any Van Gogh or Rembrandt. He was just an ordinary Joe who never did anything really important in his life."

"Then it's all just a coincidence," she insisted. "That's all. Just a coincidence."

"Fourteen coincidences? When was the last time you had a case where there were even two coincidences that really were coincidences, much less fourteen? Come on! You've been a detective for a lot of years. When have you ever seen that happen?"

Thinking for a few moments, Melanie finally shook her head. "There's got to be some other explanation, Bob. You're talking crazy stuff. I'll bet you there's information out there somewhere about this Beckwith guy, but you just forgot you saw it."

When I continued to insist that there was no large amount of information readily available on Beckwith, Melanie said she didn't want to talk about it anymore until she had done a bit of detective work herself. She insisted she would find the information about Beckwith that I had forgotten I'd seen. I was really glad to hear her say this, because I have always respected her skills as a detective, and I felt that a second, independent investigation would be a good double-check on my own work. Actually, I had kind of hoped that she would want to do this. I knew I was much too emotionally involved in the investigation, and I wanted her to check and see if it had clouded my research.

During the following two weeks, however, even though Melanie used all of her considerable detective skills and searched diligently, eventually she discovered, like me, that the information available on Beckwith proved scant at best. She found no more than what I had already found.

Now seeming completely at a loss to explain what I had found, but still reluctant to accept that what I had seen were actual memories of a past life and not just forgotten memories from this life, Melanie didn't want to talk about the subject any longer. She simply refused to be drawn into a conversation about it. However, I wouldn't let it drop. The investigation had me in its grip and wouldn't let go. Finally, I suggested to Melanie that she should visit Dr. Griffith and see for herself what I had experienced. I felt she would be much more willing to accept what I had found if she experienced something similar. At first, Melanie wouldn't even consider my suggestion, seeming to feel that if she went along with it she would be just as nutty as she thought I was. However, I wouldn't let up, and finally, more to shut me up, I believe, than to prove anything, Melanie agreed to go for a hypnotic-regression session with Dr. Griffith. I suspect that, like I had, she believed nothing of significance would happen.

For several days following her session with Dr. Griffith, Melanie appeared extremely uncomfortable about what had happened and didn't want to talk about it. I eventually found out that she had seen herself in three lives. The first past life didn't surprise me at all. For many years Melanie had been fascinated by the Civil War. We had spent several vacations hunting down and visiting Civil War sites. In one of her past lives, Melanie saw herself as an older Southern woman going to see a Union general. She was attempting to locate the whereabouts of her son, who had served in the Confederate army and had been taken prisoner. The general didn't turn out to be of much help to her.

In another life, Melanie saw herself as an Irish peasant woman. In this life, she found herself all alone with no husband or children, and when Dr. Griffith took her to her death Melanie said she saw no one around her. She died in bed by herself. Her spirit after death commented on how many times she had died alone like that.

In the third life, Melanie discovered that she was the wife of a doctor and lived in what she believed to be the American West. As her husband's duties required him to be away a lot, she again often found herself alone, and again she had no children. Although she didn't see the face of her husband in the regression, she did hear him speak, and said his voice sounded a lot like mine.

Unlike my regression, however, none of the events Melanie saw while under hypnosis had any points of reference she could work from in order to prove anything one way or the other about them. In addition, she didn't actually see anyone from her present life during her regression. The only thing she thought she recognized was the Union general, who she thought was General Burnside. Eventually, Melanie became convinced that what she had experienced had been only her imagination. She did finally admit, however, that she had no explanation for what I had found. Yet still, even with this admission, I discovered that my talking about Beckwith made her feel very uncomfortable, as if I was telling her about some secret deviant behavior.

"Okay," she cut me off one night at dinner as I was talking about something to do with Beckwith, "let's just suppose for a second that you're right about all of this past-life stuff. I'm not saying that you are, but just suppose you are. So what? What good is knowing all of this? What difference does it make?"

"It makes a hell of a lot of difference," I answered, but then after a moment realized that, in the rush of trying to find out the truth about my regression memories, I hadn't really thought much about the value of what I had found. "No one's ever done this before," I added finally, trying to give my investigation some value. "As far as I know, no one's ever had absolute proof of past-life memories before. And hell, I've got more proof than most murder cases."

"Okay, so you've got proof. Let's say you've got a ton of proof. So what? What are you going to do with it?"

Again, I realized she had brought up a topic I hadn't given much thought to. It was several moments before I answered: "To tell you the truth, I really don't know right now."

Melanie stared steadily across the table at me. "Look, Bob, you're a police captain, not some New Age nut. Let's not go talking to people about this. All right? Let's just keep this between you and me. Police captains don't believe in this sort of thing, and even if they do, they don't talk about it. I'm not saying you're wrong. I don't know. Maybe you're not. Maybe you have discovered something pretty unusual here. Okay, fine. But if you start talking about it, people are going to think you've lost your marbles."

Since I had worked in law enforcement for over a quarter of a century and knew police work to be an extremely conservative profession, I finally agreed that it probably wouldn't be a good idea to talk about what I had discovered, and we left the discussion at that. Melanie was right. Police captains were supposed to be rock solid. They were the backbone of any police department's administration. Police captains didn't get involved in, and certainly didn't go talking about, things like past lives. The next day I sent the microfilm, which I had extended once and then reordered once, back to the Archives of American Art.

CHAPTER TEN

A week or so after Melanie and I'd had our discussion and I had sent the microfilm back, I was speaking to a fellow police captain who had been one of the first people to respond to the scene of a murdered Indianapolis police officer. I knew that if I wasn't going to do anything with the Beckwith information then I needed to get back to my regular life, and I intended to use the incident involving the slain officer in one of the articles I was having published regularly in various national magazines. I asked the captain what had happened at the murder scene.

"I was one of the first officers there," the captain told me, "and you know how these kinds of situations are; it was all pretty confusing. But anyway, I ran up to where the officer was lying on the ground. I could see that his skin was already gray-looking and that his eyes were open and glazed over. So when I knelt down next to him, I knew he was already dead, but I also knew I had to try CPR anyway. When I pushed on his chest, though, I could see that his tie had been cut in half by the shotgun blast, and I suddenly realized that the shooter was still around somewhere and that he could kill me too. It was then that it happened.

"All at once, I was ten or twelve feet above the ground looking down on what was going on. I could see the top of my own head as I was trying to perform CPR. The amazing thing, though, was the total silence. I couldn't hear my radio, and I couldn't hear the other officers. I just floated up there in the silence watching what was going on. But then, after about thirty seconds or so, another officer came running up to the scene, and I suddenly went back into my body. The officer told me that the ambulance crew wouldn't come up to where we were because the shooter was still around, so we picked the officer up and carried him out to the ambulance."

I was both completely and utterly shocked and astounded by this story. The captain told me everything that happened very matter-of-factly and without any embarrassment, and apparently without any doubt that I would believe this was what had occurred. It didn't matter if it sounded weird, the captain told me. It happened.

Not long after this, I was sitting with several other officers in the federal court building in Indianapolis, waiting for my turn to testify in a federal case being heard that day. As police officers do whenever they are together, the war stories began flowing. Another police captain, who had also been called to testify, told a story about how as a young officer he had become involved in a shoot-out with some holdup men at a supermarket. My ears tingled when I heard him tell the officers about floating above his body during the shoot-out.

"My partner and I were standing in the drugstore next to the grocery," the captain said, "when this man comes running in and yelling that there's some guys with masks on holding up the grocery store. When I ran over there and went through the automatic doors, I saw one of the holdup men with a gun up to the store manager's head. All of a sudden, another holdup man in the back of the store yelled, 'Hey, that's a cop! Blow him away!' Then all hell broke loose. They started shooting, and so did I as I backed out the door as fast as I could. Bullets were flying everywhere.

"Then, all at once, I felt like I had left my body. I was floating above the parking lot outside the grocery store, and I could look down and see me and my partner shooting at the holdup men. It felt really weird. I thought maybe I had died or something, and that my soul was just wanting to see how it had happened."

Again, this captain didn't seem embarrassed by talking about his experience. When I asked him why he wasn't, he shrugged and told me, "That's what happened."

After hearing this second claim of an out-of-body experience, I wondered why I hadn't heard any of these types of stories before, but then reasoned that perhaps I had but hadn't given them much thought or credence since I'd had no similar experiences. But after hearing these two police captains tell about their experiences with no apparent fear of adverse reaction from other officers, I began making quiet, discreet inquiries around the police department concerning any other paranormal events officers had been involved in. To my shock, I found that a large number of police officers had been involved in what appeared to be paranormal events. One police sergeant, for example, told me about a run he had been on where objects in a house had moved by themselves.

"The run came out as a 'burglary in progress,'" the sergeant told me, "and since I was close by I volunteered to take it. When me and the other officer pulled up in front of the house, a woman came running out with an ice bucket lid flying out behind her. So naturally, we thought it was just another domestic disturbance. But when we asked her what the problem was, she said, 'The house is tearing itself up!'

"Well, we didn't know what to make of this, but when me and the other officer went inside, we saw that the house had been trashed. We also saw several people sitting around the kitchen table holding a crucifix and a bottle of holy water. They said, 'The house has gone crazy!'

"Then, all at once," the sergeant went on, "a vase that had been sitting on a table across the room flew over at us and smashed against the wall. Both of our jaws hit the floor. A few seconds later, a ghetto blaster flew off of a shelf and busted on the floor, then cups and saucers flew off the table. Stuff was flying everywhere. But it wasn't just things moving on their own. Eggs exploded in the refrigerator and lightbulbs would just suddenly blow up.

"To be honest with you, we really didn't know what to do, so we called the chaplain, and he and another minister came out and saw what was going on. They tried praying over the house, but that didn't seem to work. So finally they called in a Catholic priest who specializes in exorcisms, and eventually the house quieted down.

"Before all the stuff in the house finally stopped moving," the sergeant continued, "there were seven officers there who saw these things happen. The family, though, begged us not to talk to the news media about it because they knew it would bring all kinds of strange people around. And you know, after we thought about it and talked it over, we all agreed that it'd probably be better that way since everybody'd think we were nuts."

The sergeant told me that afterward, several of the television news tabloid shows contacted him. However, keeping his promise to the family, he never talked to the news media about what had happened.

Finding and listening to all of these police officers speak without reservation and without fear of being thought crazy made me believe that perhaps my own silence was unnecessary. However, I also realized that, unlike me listening to stories told by police officers to other police officers, anyone outside of law enforcement who heard about my investigation and discoveries would want more than just my word something was true. They would want undeniable proof of what I was saying. To make my case, I realized I would have to be able to answer almost every one of the twenty-eight questions I had raised about my regression experiences. I would have to have solid proof that these items were verifiably true. I knew without a doubt that this meant reading every page of Beckwith's diary from beginning to end.

Chapter Eleven

Following my discovery that a number of fellow police officers had experienced paranormal events, and as a consequence
deciding that I needed to tell my own story, I reordered the
microfilm spools from the Archives of American Art. When
I sat down at the microfilm machine, however, and looked
at the many thousands of pages involved, I knew there was
no way I could read and study Carroll Beckwith's diaries in
the short time allotted on the interlibrary loan. Even if I con-
tinuously renewed my request for the microfilm, I would still
have to wait several weeks between the time I sent the spools
back and when I could get them again by requesting another
interlibrary loan. And if anyone else needed the microfilm for
research on John Singer Sargent, William M. Chase, or someone else Beckwith knew, the wait for the spools could be even
longer. This meant that the total time necessary to read every
page of Beckwith's diaries could run up to a couple years or
maybe even longer.

That's when I came to the decision to have paper copies made of the microfilmed pages, which I could then read at home on my own schedule. However, my heart sank when I saw the result of this. The entire diary, which ran from September 10, 1871, up to the day before Beckwith died on October 24, 1917, even with several missing and short volumes, amounted to over 15,000 pages, and filled two banker's boxes. There was also a spool of photographs that I had copied, but I decided not to look at these until after I had read the diaries since I wouldn't know who the people were.

But worse than this, once I started, I found that reading Beckwith's diary turned into even more of a task than I had first imagined. It often became extremely trying and exhausting work because during some years, Beckwith used a light pencil to write in his diary, and he often scribbled. In one part of his diary, Beckwith makes the comment that when he tried to reread a diary entry from several years previous, he couldn't read his own writing. Often neither could I.

During my research of Beckwith, I also visited the Indianapolis Museum of Art specifically for the purpose of viewing the Beckwith portrait they had in storage. One morning soon after I had done this, an assistant curator at the museum, apparently hearing that I was doing research on Beckwith, called and asked for my help. She told me that they had found when they removed Beckwith's portrait of William M. Chase from its frame for cleaning that the canvas had been cut down and then re-signed by Beckwith. She asked that if during my research I found any mention of why he had done this would I please call her. Thinking that she didn't know about them, I told her about the existence of Beckwith's diaries, and that the information might be in them.

"Oh I know about the diaries," the assistant curator told me. "I tried to read them once, but they gave me such a headache."

I often felt the same way, particularly when I had to read an entry a dozen times or more, trying, because of the light pencil Beckwith used or his scribbling, to decipher what he was saying. In addition, the reading often became frustrating because a diary never gives enough information to satisfy you, using only a few sentences to record an entire day's events. Often, much is left out since the diary keeper only needs a little reminder in order to recall what happened. Beckwith would many times write a single tantalizing sentence about some important event, and then drop it, or he would make some obscure reference to what seemed to be an important matter, but then nothing else was ever said about it. In addition, he often made mention of people I hadn't heard about, with (of course) no explanation as to who they were, or he would write a short cryptic message that probably only he understood. Still, regardless of these problems, I knew the diary could be a gold mine of information because reading a diary is like having a hidden camera peeking into the most private moments of a person's life. In a diary you see the daily dramas that play out. You see the successes, the failures, the emotional encounters, and the frustrations. I knew that if I read his diary in its entirety, there existed a strong likelihood I would find and confirm most, if not all, of the items on my list.

Before I began my reading of Beckwith's diaries, I got out my list of the 28 items that could be proved or disproved about the regression session. While I had already gathered proof for 15 of the 28 items, there were three of these that I felt I needed to reconfirm or gather more proof for. First, though Beckwith said in his diary on June 16, 1875, that he drank wine while visiting Venice, Italy, I needed to know if this was just a one-time event or if he was a lifelong wine drinker. I felt my proof about him ordering the glass of wine at the sidewalk cafe, as I saw him do during the hypnotic regression, would be more solid if he regularly drank wine, which would then solidly confirm item #13. I also felt I had only partly confirmed item #6, concerning Bertha going to France with him. Although I had found a short biography that said the Beckwiths spent many summers in Europe, I needed a specific reference to France.

In addition to these two items, I also needed to find an entry in Beckwith's diaries that mentioned him painting the portrait of the hunchbacked woman, the portrait I had found in the art gallery in New Orleans. This became necessary because once I discovered that I had apparently stumbled onto something tremendously significant, I returned to New Orleans with the intention of obtaining a photograph of the painting or perhaps even purchasing it if I could get it at a good price (closer to $1,000 than the original asking price of $5,000). However, instead I got a surprise.

When I got back to New Orleans, I found that the art gallery I had seen the painting in had gone out of business. Not knowing what else to do, I simply did what any detective would have done and began canvassing nearby art galleries to see if I could find someone who knew what had happened to the painting. An art dealer a block or so from the out-of-business art gallery told me that several things could have happened to the paintings that had been at the gallery, but most likely they were sold or consigned to another gallery in New Orleans. However, following this, I encountered the same problem I'd had when I first began my investigation and was searching for the two paintings I'd seen in my regression—there was no central registry of paintings. In other words, if a person wanted to buy a Beckwith painting, there was nowhere to check in order to find out which art gallery or art dealer had one for sale. A person simply had to begin calling or visiting art dealers and galleries.

That is basically what I did. I obtained a list of all the art dealers in New Orleans and then began visiting each one, asking if they had seen the portrait in question. After several days of searching, I finally located the art dealer who had obtained the portrait from the out-of-business gallery and had displayed it in his own gallery. Unfortunately, I also found out that he had sold it. I then discovered an important fact about the art world: art dealers religiously protect the privacy of their clients. Even though I explained that all I needed was a photograph of the portrait, the art dealer wouldn't tell me anything about who he had sold the painting to. He insisted that the only thing he could do was pass my name, address, and telephone number along to the owner, and then, if the owner wished, he or she could contact me. With no other recourse, I left that information with the art dealer, but never heard from the owner. So consequently, I knew I needed to find some other verification, beyond just my word, that this painting existed, and I hoped to find it in the diaries.

I decided after coming back from New Orleans that I probably should tell my two children what I was doing before someone else did. My son, much like his mother, didn't believe it and insisted (and still does to this day) that I had come by the facts about Beckwith somewhere in this life. My daughter would later tell me that she was kind of shocked when I told her about seeing her in one of my regressions and that she didn't know what to think. Interestingly enough, when I told her about Beckwith, she asked me if he had a father or brother named Charley. She said it was just something that came to her. Beckwith's father's name was Charles, as was one of Beckwith's brothers. But overall, my investigation of Carroll Beckwith had little impact on my relationship with my children. At this time, they were going through the period in their youth in which they had minimal interest in their parents' affairs, being much more concerned about the affairs of their peer group.

Now that my family knew what I was doing, I began my reading of Beckwith's diaries one afternoon when I was home by myself and had all day free. I gathered a highlighter, a notepad, and a large magnifying glass (which proved very handy many times). With a tingling of excitement running through my hands, I opened the top banker's box, pulled out the first volume, dated September 10, 1871, and began reading.

Carroll Beckwith, I discovered, began his diary with the enthusiasm and exuberance typical of a boy just a few weeks away from his nineteenth birthday. Actually, at first Beckwith's diary more resembles a journal, with his first entry being a rambling account of the time he had spent with his mother in various areas around Oxford, New York. The second entry, which runs for eleven pages, talks about, among other things, the death of his grandmother. Naturally, I wondered if this could be the woman who had died of a blood clot and had affected me so deeply during the regression. However, Beckwith said in his diary that his grandmother didn't recognize anyone at the last, and that he felt good because she was finally out of her suffering, as she had apparently been in great pain for some time. His entry just didn't seem to give his grandmother the significance that I felt the woman who had died of a blood clot would have had in his life.

The fourth entry in Beckwith's diary vividly describes a pivotal event in his life: the Chicago fire of October 1871, which not only destroyed the family home and business, but also finally forced his father to relent and agree to allow him to pursue art as a career.

From the very first page, I found the diary intensely interesting because I knew that no one in history had likely ever had an opportunity such as this—an opportunity to read a daily account of a previous life. Reading Beckwith's diary, I realized, would be like reliving his life day by day in five- or six-sentence segments.

Soon, though, I discovered that for the first few years Beckwith kept his diary, it was a hit-and-miss project, with entries made only occasionally. Beckwith left Chicago to study art in New York City, became sick with rheumatism and had to return home, and then, after recovering, returned to New York City. Finally, in October 1873, Beckwith sailed for France, where he intended to further his art studies. Being accepted in the school of painter Carolus-Duran, he made friends with fellow art student John Singer Sargent, and they took an apartment together. All of the above incidents are told in diary entries often made months apart.

In October 1878, Beckwith completed his art training and returned to the United States. The next year, Beckwith accepted a teaching position at the Art Students' League in New York City. From this point on, he began making regular daily entries into his diary, which, with only a few exceptions, he continued until his death almost forty years later, a total of well over 14,000 pages. And while I found all of the entries about Beckwith's life fascinating, I still watched for any entries that could confirm the remaining items on my list of facts.

It didn't take me long to reconfirm item #8, that Beckwith, as I said during my regression, didn't like to paint portraits. The reason soon became obvious. He had absolutely no confidence in his ability to paint portraits. Hundreds of times in his diaries,

Beckwith talked about how poor his ability was in bringing a likeness of the person to the canvas, how his portraits always lacked life and vitality, and how depressed his finished portraits made him. However, I don't think that Beckwith's lack of confidence was obvious to anyone but him because he was often described in the short biographies I found as a very competent and popular portrait painter. Interestingly, he felt this lack of confidence even though he also mentioned many times in his diaries how pleased his customers told him they were with his portraits, and even though he often received good notices in the newspapers about portraits he had on exhibition.

The diaries also quickly confirmed another thing I said during my regression, item #9, that Beckwith didn't like painting portraits, but he needed the money. In his diaries, Beckwith kept a detailed record of *every* cent he earned. From these entries, it can clearly be seen that during his life Beckwith received a major portion of his income from portrait painting. And even though he occasionally made money from painting subjects other than portraits, the amount proved insignificant by comparison. The fact was, without portraits, Beckwith couldn't have made a living as a painter.

In confirming item #14, I found Beckwith's diaries filled with hundreds and hundreds of entries about his desperate need for money. This appeared to be the major motivation of his life. No matter what kind of year he had financially, Beckwith seemed to never feel that he was making enough or had enough money. This also answered item #17. If Beckwith and his wife fought, and I've never known of a married couple who didn't, it would have been over money. Beckwith had an obsession about it. In his diary, he kept a record of not just every cent he earned, but also every cent he spent. Whenever he traveled, he always searched for the cheapest hotels, and if he had to buy something he thought was expensive, he would record the amount he paid in his diary, followed by "!!!" In his diaries, he also kept detailed records of how much he spent for gloves, for lunches, for models, and even for things as small as a head of lettuce. Money was the driving force throughout his life, and undoubtedly would have been the source of any arguments he and Bertha had.

While a large number of the daily entries that Beckwith made concerned money, other entries told about such mundane things such as which model posed for him, which club he ate dinner in, and who he saw that day, all of which made for slow, boring reading since I many times had to decipher the entries first. Occasionally, however, I would come across a gem that related to my regression. For example, while under hypnosis, I saw myself walking with a cane. However, I told Dr. Griffith that it wasn't because I was old and needed assistance walking, but rather I was using a fancy walking stick. Although in his youth Beckwith had suffered through several severe bouts of rheumatism, these didn't seem to affect his ability to walk long distances as an adult. For instance, in his diaries, Beckwith often mentioned visiting relatives on Sunday by walking from his apartment on 57th Street up to 85th

Street, and then on up to 115th Street. A walking stick, therefore, would have been a likely item he would have possessed, and I found that he did. Three places in his diaries, December 20, 1882; October, 18, 1910; and March 9, 1915; Beckwith wrote about using or receiving the present of a walking stick, which confirmed item #12. I also found several photographs of Beckwith with a fancy walking stick. These walking sticks were usually much too thin to support any weight, so they had to be for show.

During one scene in my regression, I found myself arguing with someone about the poor lighting for a painting of mine that was being exhibited. As I found out by reading Beckwith's diaries, picture hanging for an art show was a complex and critically important part of any exhibition. Exhibition planners often formed hanging committees who decided which paintings were hung where, and consequently which paintings got the spots with the best lighting and exposure. I found through reading Beckwith's diaries that there was often deep resentment from painters who felt they had gotten a bad hanging. I discovered nine different entries in Beckwith's diaries that told of him being upset and "having a row" over a bad picture hanging or lighting, which confirmed item #15.

When I first began my search for evidence that I hoped would prove my hypnotic regression was just my imagination or maybe forgotten memories, I felt that the scene where I saw myself in the late 1800s or early 1900s drinking wine could be the key to doing this. I had hoped I would find that

Beckwith was a teetotaler, but, if not, I was under the impression that during this era few men drank wine; rather, most men who drank alcohol drank whiskey. However, I found in reading his diaries that Beckwith made many comments about his love of good wine. He once recorded a diary entry about how people looked upon him as being a bit strange because of his taste for wine, but that he had acquired this taste while living in France. Several times in his diaries, Beckwith complained about attending dinners where no wine was served, all of which reconfirmed item #13.

Another important incident that occurred while I was under hypnosis, and which I felt early on could prove that my regression likely wasn't true, was when I said, "She died of a blood clot. They said a blood clot killed her." At the time I said this, I didn't know who I was talking about, only that whoever this person was she had been supremely important in my life. I had felt like I wanted to cry. I reasoned that if my regression memory was valid, then some woman very important in Beckwith's life had to have died from a blood clot. I knew that if I could find no woman important to him who had died from a blood clot, this would do serious damage to the validity of my regression memory. After reading his diaries, I knew that for Carroll Beckwith there were only two women who fit this description: first his mother, whom he devotes page after page in his diaries to, talking of his love for her, and later, his wife, Bertha. Item #24, I judged, could be the deciding factor as to whether or not what I experienced under hypnosis had any validity.

And so, when in my reading I got to December 5, 1886, I suddenly stopped and felt chills run up and down both sides of my neck. On that day, Beckwith records, his mother attended church, and while there suffered a stroke, caused by a blood clot. She died later that day. After I read this entry, I felt very similar to the way I had felt in New Orleans when I stumbled onto the portrait of the hunchbacked woman. Much like finding the portrait, this entry hit me like an unexpected slap in the face. This was undeniable evidence that what I had seen while under hypnosis had been scenes from Carroll Beckwith's life. How else could I have known this?

For the scene during my regression in which I found myself at some type of party or reception where I was being honored and congratulated, I found several entries in Beckwith's diaries that recorded this, and which confirmed item #7. On March 31, 1879, Beckwith writes in his diary several sentences about a reception at which crowds of people congratulated him. On May 11, 1889, he writes about another reception in which he found himself surrounded by people congratulating him, and of how the newspapers, without exception, highly praised his work.

Rechecking my list, I found that one of the unconfirmed items I still had left concerned a statement I had made while under hypnosis: I didn't think my wife could have children. On October 24, 1888, coincidentally twenty-nine years to the day before Beckwith would die, he reports in his diary that Bertha suffered an extremely difficult miscarriage. After this incident, though Beckwith makes a few mentions in his diaries about how envious he is of couples who can have children, he and Bertha remain childless for the remainder of their lives, which confirmed items #19 and #20.

As a follow-up to the above two items, I also said while under hypnosis that my wife and I were happy even though we didn't have children. Were the Beckwiths? After reading his diaries, I felt very confident that, at least for Carroll, their marriage was everything he wanted it to be. Many times in his diaries, he spoke of his love and admiration for Bertha and how happy he was that he married her, confirming item #21.

During one part of my regression, I saw myself painting the hunchbacked woman in a studio that seemed to have a huge number of windows and a large skylight. I also told Dr. Griffith earlier in the regression that my studio was filled with unsold paintings. In 1912, after returning to the United States from Europe, Beckwith and his wife moved into the Schuyler Hotel on West 45th Street in New York City. In his diary on September 9, 1912, Beckwith describes his studio at the Schuyler Hotel as having a wall of solid windows and a large skylight, which confirmed item #22. Five times in his diary (on June 5, 1907; March 14, 1908; April 21, 1908; May 27, 1909; and October 25, 1912), Beckwith comments about the large number of unsold paintings he had hanging and stored in his studio, which confirmed item #25. More important though, since this reconfirmed a crucial piece of my evidence, three times in his diary of 1912, on October 18, November 23, and December 28,

Beckwith writes about painting the portrait of a hunchbacked woman in his studio at the Schuyler Hotel, which reconfirmed item #1.

After finding confirmation after confirmation and no longer having any doubt at all that what I had seen while under hypnosis were actual scenes from Carroll Beckwith's life, I really threw myself into reading the diary, often, to my wife's chagrin, spending up to ten hours a day on weekends. I was now convinced that I would eventually find confirmation for every item on my list, and that I wasn't going to find the disproving fact. When looking over my list after checking off that I had reconfirmed item #1, the existence of the hunchbacked woman's portrait, I found that I had only five of the items left to confirm.

Two of these items came from an experience I'd had during my regression in which I saw myself walking into a house and finding Bertha playing the piano. I told Dr. Griffith I believed I was in France. In his diaries, Beckwith tells of many trips he and Bertha made to France, which confirmed item #6. He also tells of having a piano in their apartment in New York City and in their summer home in the Catskills. But did Bertha play the piano, and would she play it for others? Yes. Beckwith writes often in his diaries about Bertha either playing the piano or singing for friends, which confirmed item #18.

As I checked these two items off of my list, I looked at the three items I still needed proof for. These were the statements I made while in the hypnotic regression that I was a good artist but it took so long, that I was happy when I painted, and that people didn't like me but did like my paintings.

While reading Beckwith's diaries, I at first wondered if he ever thought he was a good artist, given his constant gloominess over what he believed was a lack of talent compared to other artists. However, I found that in the last few years of his life, starting about 1914, Beckwith began to have a much better opinion of his talent, one time even stating that no artist in America could match his talent in portraits. Indeed, it did take a long time for him to finally believe he was a good artist, which confirmed item #26.

Beckwith also stated many times in his diaries, given that he was so often set upon by periods of depression, that he was happiest when he was painting, confirming item #27.

And finally, as for item #28, the statement I made that people didn't like me but liked my paintings, this also appeared difficult to believe because for most of his life Beckwith seemed to be a very outgoing, amicable fellow with dozens of friends. However, Beckwith's diaries began showing a distinct change in his personality, starting around 1912, when he notes that Bertha scolded him for his rudeness to others. This is followed by later entries of more mentions of Bertha's belief that he had become a grouchy old man. Beckwith also recorded several instances of him being so sharp that he made women cry and had diary entries about his sudden dislike for leaving their apartment for social engagements. This is in strong contrast to a man who for over thirty years had been a veritable social butterfly, going out several times a week to dinners, receptions, plays, the opera, and other such places.

An incident in 1910, I discovered, also added to his personality change. Before making his move to Rome in that year, Beckwith held a large sale of his work in the hope that its proceeds would finance his trip. He became very bitter, and remained so until he died, over the fact that a large number of people he thought were his friends didn't show up for the sale. But even more indicative of a personality change, on February 12, 1913, Beckwith made his first diary entry critical of John Singer Sargent, a man he had viewed as his most intimate friend for forty years. In addition to all of this, Beckwith was part of the art world during a time of radical changes. He, however, refused to accept any of these changes, and instead referred to Impressionists, cubists, modern-art adherents, and others seeking to introduce new concepts into the art world as gangs of dangerous revolutionaries. His stern opposition to any changes likely made him few friends. Indeed, at the last of his life, a lot of people probably didn't like Carroll Beckwith, confirming item #28.

When I finished the last diary entry Beckwith made on October 23, 1917, I realized, after a year of research on the diaries, that I had now proven beyond even the smallest doubt that I carried memories of Carroll Beckwith in my mind. There was no other explanation. With the level of proof I had, if this had been a criminal case, I would have been absolutely certain of a conviction.

Regardless of this, and even though I had decided to earlier, I still felt very nervous and anxious about going public with what I had discovered. And while I would often tell myself that the truth was the truth and that I shouldn't be frightened of telling it, at other times I wondered if I ought, as Melanie still advised, to just keep my discoveries to myself. I realized that making claims such as I would be doing likely wouldn't be looked upon favorably by many people, both inside and outside of law enforcement. And even though I had found that a large number of other police officers had experienced paranormal events, I also found that most of them hadn't told anyone besides other police officers and close family members. If I went public with my discoveries, I would be telling the world.

I also realized that, because my claims were so unconventional, a large number of people, regardless of the overwhelming evidence I presented, would deny that what I claimed could be true. Many wouldn't even want to look at my proof, but would simply dismiss me as being just another one of those "odd people" who believed in reincarnation. I wasn't really sure I wanted to be thought of as a part of that group. Yet, at the same time, I realized, with the exception of Cathy Graban and Dr. Griffith, I didn't actually know anyone who believed in past lives, and I couldn't be certain that these two women were representative of the people who did. Perhaps, I considered, I should meet a bunch of these people before I went public with my discoveries. Maybe I should see if I wanted to be associated with people who believed in past lives.

During my research, I had come across the fact several times that there existed a group of mental health professionals called the Association for Past-Life Research and Therapies (APRT). According to what I read, this was supposed to be a group of psychologists and psychiatrists who regularly used past-life regression therapy in their practice and who had formed this organization in order to spread information and encourage training in the use of past-life regression therapy. But while that was interesting, what I really needed to know was whether these were just normal, ordinary mental health professionals who had discovered a therapy that worked, or a group of people I really didn't want to be associated with. I decided that I needed to meet and speak with members of APRT before I went public with my findings.

CHAPTER TWELVE

Once I decided what I needed to do before I went public, I went back and looked through some of the information I had gathered during my early investigation. I remembered seeing the mailing address of the Association for Past-Life Research and Therapies. Finding it, I sent them a letter inquiring about their next gathering or conference, thinking that this would be the most expedient way of meeting a large number of APRT members. Speaking with members of this organization at a conference would tell me whether I wanted to be lumped in with this group or if I would just take my information about Beckwith to the grave. Also, I thought that going to a large gathering like this would likely allow me to stay anonymous. Depending on what I found out about the members of APRT, this, I decided, might be an excellent option.

I received a packet of information from APRT in the mail a week or so later and discovered that they had a conference planned in just two months in Fort Lauderdale, Florida. This seemed almost too perfect since Melanie had been wanting to go to Fort Lauderdale for some time, as her father resided in a nursing home there. So, I sent APRT a check and registered for the conference, but didn't mention that I was a police captain or that I was investigating a past-life regression. I definitely intended to go there incognito. That way, I figured, if APRT turned out to be a collection of people on the fringe, I could simply slip away.

When the day of the conference rolled around, Melanie and I boarded a plane early in the morning, and two hours later stepped off in Florida. Immediately upon our arrival at our hotel in Fort Lauderdale, the Crown Sterling Suites, I didn't go out to see the ocean or other sites, but instead hurried down to the conference area and picked up my registration information. While the people handing out the material seemed normal enough, I figured that didn't mean anything since they were more likely hotel employees than members of APRT.

Carrying the information back to our room and looking it over, I found there was a "get acquainted" cocktail hour that evening, which seemed like an excellent opportunity to begin my evaluation of the conference participants. I had hoped that Melanie would go to this function with me since a couple can circulate easier, and I also wanted her opinion of the attendees. She, however, still didn't feel comfortable about what I had found or what I proposed to do with it. She had admitted she couldn't prove me wrong or come up with an alternate explanation, but still she didn't want to commit herself by going to the conference. She said she would go to the nursing home instead.

Later that evening, even though I had tried to prepare myself all afternoon, I felt a bit nervous as I walked alone into the "get acquainted" cocktail hour. I wasn't certain what questions to ask the people I spoke to or what I would tell them if they asked me who I was or why I was there. Fortunately, I found the room crowded, which made being inconspicuous easier, and so I began circulating, saying hello and entering into small talk with the people there. One of the lecturers at the conference, I quickly found out, was also named Snow, so I think many of the people there must have thought that he and I were connected somehow, though I had never met him before that night. With that, I had no problem moving about and mixing, and no one asked about my reason for being there.

To my relief, I found that the large majority of the people I talked with that evening seemed to be rational individuals with no obvious signs of severe psychological problems. I did find a few strange, and a couple of very strange, people at the conference, but this didn't surprise me. I had assumed that the topic would attract a certain number of odd people. One of these individuals, for example, told me that her job was preparing the human race for the imminent arrival of benevolent aliens who would wipe away all of Earth's problems, while another claimed he talked regularly with the ghost of

Napoleon. Fortunately, none of these people, I discovered upon talking with them, were members of APRT, but were simply lay individuals who had been drawn to the conference by its topic. And, I had to admit to myself, before I began the investigation into my past-life regression I would have lumped anyone who believed in reincarnation in with these people. So I knew I couldn't be real judgmental since I now belonged to that group. When the cocktail hour ended and I returned to my room that night, I felt much more comfortable than I had when I arrived.

Two months earlier, when I had received my packet of conference information in the mail, I found that there were a large selection of workshops I could attend, from "Treating Mental Illness Using Past-Life Regression Therapy" to "Regression Techniques: Finding Your Life's Purpose" to "The Vision of the Third Eye." I signed up for as many of these workshops as I could attend, not for what I could learn about using past-life-regression therapy as a psychological tool, but to meet as many mental health professionals as possible who apparently believed in past lives.

The first two members of APRT I met at these workshops were Robert Jarmon, MD, a psychiatrist who used past-life regression therapy in his practice, and who interestingly enough was a psychiatric consultant to the Roman Catholic Church in central New Jersey; and Linda Adler, a licensed clinical social worker and psychotherapist, who at that time was vice president of APRT, and eventually became its president.

Both of these individuals I found to be sincere, caring professionals who were simply willing to use a therapy that others might consider questionable because they found it worked and helped their patients. I also spoke with the president of APRT, Bettye Binder, and a large number of other mental health professionals who taught the workshops, including Dr. Chet Snow.

From my many years in law enforcement, I had developed the talent of being able to detect very quickly when a person is walking on the edge of reality. A police officer's life often depends on this skill. That description, however, didn't fit any members of APRT that I met. Instead, all of the members I met appeared to be sincere, compassionate individuals who were more concerned about the welfare of their patients than flouting convention. When I left the conference several days later, I felt much more comfortable about being lumped in with this group of people.

As a result, when I returned home, I immediately began preparing to go public. However, before I could do this, I knew there was one more bit of information I needed to investigate. During my reading of Beckwith's diaries, I found that he often mentioned working on his scrapbooks, which I eventually discovered resided at the New-York Historical Society. I also discovered that these scrapbooks hadn't been microfilmed and, because of their fragility, they were not available for inter-library loan. They could only be viewed in the Society's head-quarters at 77th and Central Park West in New York City.

There were three reasons I had to examine these scrapbooks. First, I wanted to satisfy my own desire to see and
touch something that Beckwith had handled often during
his life. Second, there had cropped up a minor incongruity
about one piece of the evidence I had uncovered. According
to the reports I found, Beckwith died at around 5:00 p.m. on
October 24, 1917. However, in my regression, when I rose
above the city after my death, it had appeared dark, probably
several hours later than this. While I realized this was a very
minor point, I also realized that what I proposed to go public
with would not be readily accepted by many people, and that
these people would look for any minor anomaly like this. I
hoped the scrapbooks, which reportedly included one kept
by Bertha that I figured might contain information about
Beckwith's death, would clear up this point. Lastly, while I
couldn't imagine that after not finding anything to disprove
my regression in his diaries I would find any such thing in his
scrapbooks, I knew I couldn't finish up a proper investigation
without examining this critical piece of evidence.

The scrapbooks, though, were actually only part of the reason I needed to go to New York City. On his death certificate,
it stated that Beckwith had been buried at Kensico Cemetery
in Valhalla, New York, which is just north of New York City.
Although I realized I didn't have to visit the grave in order to
properly complete this investigation, and every time I thought
about it my stomach would cramp up like it was full of wet hay,
the thought of being able to visit my own grave seemed almost
too tempting to pass up.

CHAPTER THIRTEEN

After checking into the Empire Radisson Hotel on 63rd Street in New York City, I asked the desk clerk for directions and then walked up to the New-York Historical Society at 77th and Central Park West. In Indianapolis, a block is approximately a tenth of a mile, and so I had figured that the walk to the Historical Society from 63rd and Columbus would be close to two miles. I happily discovered that the blocks between the east/west streets in Manhattan are much less than a tenth of a mile, and so what I had believed would be a hike turned into a casual stroll.

The New-York Historical Society sat across the street from the American Museum of Natural History and resided in a four-story limestone building adjacent to Central Park. Upon arriving, I didn't have time to admire the area, so I immediately walked up the steps and inside. I paid the $5.00 admittance fee and asked the attendant for directions to the library, which she said was on the second floor. While I had imagined it being much larger, considering their resources and subject matter, when I stepped into the room, I found the Historical Society's library to be quite small.

The librarian, after I walked up to the counter and asked her for Carroll Beckwith's scrapbooks, handed me a request slip and then directed me to a collection of old wooden cabinets. They reminded me of the cabinets that had stood for decades in the Brightwood Public Library, where my mother had always taken me as a child, cabinets that contained the Dewey decimal cards. Indeed, that was basically what these cabinets were, and, after finding the card for James Carroll Beckwith, I noted the reference number of his scrapbooks on the request slip. However, when I handed the slip back to the librarian a few moments later, she asked, "You want them all?"

I had imagined from the references Beckwith made in his diaries to the scrapbooks that there would be just two or three of them. So I nodded.

A few minutes later, however, a young library assistant rolled a cart over to my table. On it I found six large and two small scrapbooks, all appearing completely full. I immediately realized that hundreds of pages would need to be read and examined, and I suddenly wondered about the wisdom of giving myself only four days to do this research, particularly since the library at the Historical Society stayed open for only six hours a day.

After the library assistant gave me a short course on how to handle the obviously old and fragile scrapbooks, he gently

placed scrapbook number one (Beckwith had numbered the
six large scrapbooks and also noted on their covers the dates
of their contents) into a protective stand on the table. I looked
for a few moments at the scrapbook. While I didn't think I
was going to find anything startling in Beckwith's scrapbooks
after already reading over forty years of his diary, I knew that
a person's scrapbook gives you insight into that person's values and what he or she found most important during his or
her life. What a person pastes into a scrapbook are memories
that he or she values highly and never wants to forget. When I
touched the cover of the scrapbook to open it, I felt a tingling
that raced up to my shoulder. Whether this was just anticipation or something else I didn't know, but I felt certain that,
while perhaps they wouldn't surprise me, these scrapbooks
should give me even more insight into the man whose diary I
had been reading for the last year.

What I found as I opened the cover and began reviewing the contents of the scrapbook was every newspaper and
magazine article that Beckwith's name had appeared in,
including not only American newspapers and magazines but
foreign ones as well. Beckwith, I discovered, though he had
never mentioned this in his diary, had employed several clipping services to locate and send him the articles from around
the world. This proved fortunate for me and made examining the scrapbooks easier because it meant that often a dozen
or more of the articles pasted in the scrapbook covered the
same incident, and many times were identical, but had simply

appeared in different magazines or newspapers. Beckwith also included in his scrapbooks many of the reviews he had received on his work, most of which, contrary to the defeatist attitude in his diary entries, were favorable to very favorable about his painting. Several of them called Beckwith "America's finest and most popular portrait painter." I also found glued in the scrapbooks copies of letters Beckwith had had published in various newspapers concerning the many charitable causes he had become involved with during his life, as well as his many letters to newspapers condemning what he saw as radical and dangerous changes in the art world. I was particularly pleased though to find a number of photographs filling the pages, both of his more popular paintings and of the people and places I had read so much about in his diaries. Finally, I found the remaining spaces in the scrapbooks filled with incidental documents such as passports, letters of credit, and hotel bills.

After spending two full six-hour days going through the scrapbooks, which, because of the duplication of items included in them, turned out to be an easier task than I had first thought, I didn't come across much new information that Beckwith's diaries hadn't provided. I did, however, find eight articles from eight different newspapers about an incident I believe was likely the one I had experienced during my hypnotic regression in which I saw myself having an argument with someone concerning the hanging of one of my paintings, which was item #15 on my list. For some reason, considering the space he gave to it in his scrapbook, this incident had been very important to Beckwith. It was even reported in the *Paris Herald* of February 5, 1913, in an article titled: "Artist, Indignant, Takes Portrait from Clubhouse." According to the articles in the scrapbook, Beckwith became so incensed about the bad hanging and poor lighting for a portrait he had lent to the Catholic Club in New York City that he had a scene with the club operators and finally took his painting off of the wall and carried it home with him.

In addition to the above, I also found in the scrapbook a photograph of Bertha playing the piano with a number of friends standing around, which added more evidence to fact #18. During my regression, I heard piano music coming from inside a house as I walked in the garden. When I stepped into the house, I saw Bertha playing the piano.

I found that Bertha had added some things to scrapbook number 6, Beckwith's final scrapbook, after his death. (One of the two, small, unnumbered scrapbooks was Beckwith's first scrapbook; the other unnumbered one belonged to Bertha and contained articles about the causes she had been involved in.) Bertha, apparently continuing to use the clipping services, accumulated and pasted in scrapbook #6 over fifty of Carroll Beckwith's obituary notices from newspapers all over the world. From these, I cleared up a small discrepancy that I had found between the facts I had gathered on Beckwith and what I had seen during my hypnotic regression. The reports I had gathered all agreed that Beckwith had died of a heart attack in New York City on October 24, 1917, at about 5:00 p.m. In New York City, however, even late in October, it isn't nearly as dark at this hour as I experienced in my regression when I rose above the city. It appeared to be several hours later than this.

One of the obituaries, which appeared in the *New York Herald* on October 25, 1917, went into great detail about Beckwith's death, stating that neither he nor Bertha had any inkling he had heart problems, and that Beckwith had been feeling well until the day of his fatal heart attack. That day, according to Bertha's entries in Beckwith's diary, they had been making plans to travel to Cleveland to review an exhibition of Beckwith's work scheduled to be held there. His sudden and completely unexpected death obviously staggered and dumbfounded Bertha. Consequently, she was so overcome by the shock of having her husband return home and die in her arms that she had an attack of her own and had to have medical attention. Considering the deep love he expressed for Bertha throughout his diaries, I believe Beckwith's soul very likely stayed with Bertha until she recovered, which would account for the missing hours before I rose above the darkened city.

On the last pages of Carroll Beckwith's final scrapbook, Bertha also pasted articles that told about his funeral. According to the articles, the funeral, held at St. Thomas's Church in New York City, drew many members of New York's artistic community, along with many of the city's high society. Another article Bertha pasted into the scrapbook told about a bust of Beckwith that had been placed in the Gould Memorial Library at New York University.

When I finally closed the last scrapbook at the end of my second day, I knew that, beyond already having proved 26 of the 28 facts I had started out to prove (with item #11, Beckwith using the name Jack, being only a probable confirmation, and item #16, Beckwith's wife's name being Amanda, being a miss), I had now added even more proof to the proof I already had. But more important, I hadn't found any evidence that could disprove the things I had seen during my hypnotic regression. Beckwith's wife's name not being Amanda didn't really affect the proof I had gathered because when I said it during the regression I knew it wasn't right.

I felt strangely saddened when the library announced it was closing for the day and the attendant wheeled the cart with the scrapbooks away. Through my examination of Beckwith's scrapbooks, diaries, and autobiography, I had now reviewed his total life, and I thought about what that life had meant, and what I ought to have learned from it. I turned this all over in my mind as I left the Historical Society and headed for my hotel.

The most obvious lesson I could see from Beckwith's life was that a person must learn to accept change that is inevitable, and not oppose it simply because it isn't what has always been done. Beckwith was part of the art world at a time when major changes were occurring, but he refused to embrace any of them and instead clung to his traditional view of art. During Beckwith's life, modern art, the Cubist movement, Impressionism, and other radical departures from traditional art suddenly sprang onto the scene. However, because Beck-with vigorously opposed all of them, he was left behind by contemporaries such as William M. Chase, John Singer Sargent, Claude Monet, and others who adapted and embraced change. As a result, Chase, Sargent, and Monet all have books written about them, and their paintings are worth a fortune, while Beckwith's legacy largely died with him.

I knew I faced a similar situation in my own life. I was facing a huge change in how I viewed the universe. Life apparently didn't operate as I had always thought it did, and I was going to have to embrace and accept these changes. Considering how radical these changes were, I could relate and sympathize with Beckwith's struggle.

A second important lesson I could see from Beckwith's life was that a person should not pursue and desire money as desperately as he did. This trait, I found, actually made his life worse than it should have been, because he was never happy, no matter how much money he made or had. For example, when the uncle he had lived with while studying art in New York City died and left him $10,000, a huge sum in the late 1800s, Beckwith wasn't happy or elated about it. Instead, his diary entries show him becoming increasing bitter in later years because he always felt he should have gotten more. Beck-with's diaries are filled with hundreds and hundreds of entries about his desperate desire to have and make more money, even though, interestingly enough, during the last decade of his life Beckwith was actually fairly well off financially. However, a person would never think so considering the woes recorded in his diaries. I felt very fortunate that I apparently hadn't carried this trait of Beckwith's with me into this life.

As I walked back to my hotel after finishing my work at the Historical Society, I thought about another research project I had considered doing while I was in New York. In my research I had found that, even though the Beckwiths had a family cemetery in Illinois, Bertha had buried her husband at Kensico Cemetery in Valhalla, New York, which is a suburb of New York City. And though while safely back in Indianapolis it had seemed like an exciting idea to visit the grave, now that I was just a few miles from it, the idea didn't sound quite as good. For an unexplained reason, I felt anxious and uncertain. But yet, I asked myself as I strolled down Central Park West, how could I be this close and not visit the grave? After all, how many people get to knowingly visit their graves while they are still alive? This had to be a first. Even so, the thought of doing it dried my throat and sent icy waves of electricity through me.

The next day, having two days left in New York City, I decided to visit the places Beckwith had lived and worked, putting off going to his grave, if I did go, until the final day. As I traveled from site to site that afternoon, I found that almost all of the locations I looked for were no longer there. Much of the New York City of Carroll Beckwith is gone. The Sherwood Studio Building, where Beckwith lived and worked for many years, no longer exists. The site where the apartment building stood that he and Bertha lived in for a time on East

58th Street is now occupied by a huge office skyscraper, while a small park now occupies the site of the Schuyler Hotel, where Beckwith died. I did find, interestingly enough, that the Art Students' League, where Beckwith served as a teacher for nearly twenty years, now has its headquarters in the former home of the American Fine Arts Society on West 57th Street, just two blocks from where Beckwith's home and studio in the Sherwood Studio Building had been.

When I returned to my hotel that night, I felt saddened that practically everything Beckwith knew in New York City had disappeared. At the same time though, my stomach cramped at the thought of what I might do the next day.

CHAPTER FOURTEEN

August 1999

After I wavered back and forth the previous evening about
going to the graveyard, several times deciding yes and several
times no, the morning of my final day in New York City I got
out of bed early, dressed, and took a cab to Grand Central Station before I had time to think about what I was doing and
perhaps back out. Having been a police officer for thirty years,
I knew that what I was experiencing was fear, and I knew how
to deal with it. You use your experiences with similar events
to examine what you're afraid of, consider all of the variables
involved in your present situation, and then decide how you
will handle each of these variables. Doing this greatly dilutes
the fear because there are few unknowns left. In this situation, however, that didn't work. I had no idea what any of the
variables were because this situation was totally unique in my
experience. Even so, I kept telling myself that being frightened

about visiting a grave was something that eleven-year-olds did, not police captains. I was just letting my imagination run wild.

Climbing out of the cab, I walked into the train terminal and soon found out where the expression "as crowded as Grand Central Station" comes from. Although at first dismayed at the sight of all the people waiting to buy a ticket, I found that the long lines at the ticket windows moved fairly quickly. I waited only a few minutes before stepping up to the window and purchasing a ticket on the Metro-North Railroad Harlem Line for Valhalla, New York.

I didn't want to stand around and think about what I was about to do, so I passed the short wait for the train by looking around Grand Central Station, admiring for several minutes the Zodiac painted on the ceiling in the main lobby, then hurrying and boarding the train at the last minute. Following a fairly pleasant, thirty-five-minute ride in an only half-filled car, I stepped off of the train and felt as if I could have been back in Indiana. The quiet little town of Valhalla gave no clue that it sat so close to one of the world's largest cities. However, as I walked from the train platform, I realized that, though I knew Kensico Cemetery was in Valhalla, I didn't know exactly where in Valhalla it was, so I walked over to a nearby deli to get directions. The graveyard turned out to be only a short distance away, and, the weather being pleasant, I enjoyed the walk.

When I arrived at the office of the graveyard, the lady I spoke with there proved to be extremely helpful. She highlighted a plot map of Kensico, showing me exactly where

Beckwith's grave was, and then gave me a rather intricate map, on which she highlighted the route from the office to the grave site. A brochure she also handed me noted that a number of famous people had been buried at Kensico Cemetery, including actor Danny Kaye, writer Ayn Rand, baseball great Lou Gehrig, band leader Tommy Dorsey, and radio operator David Sarnoff. While this last name may not sound familiar, he was the radio operator who picked up the distress call that the ocean liner *Titanic* had collided with an iceberg and was sinking.

While I couldn't tell the distance to Beckwith's grave since I didn't know the exact scale of the map, I thanked the lady for her help and then started out again on foot. Kensico Cemetery, I discovered as I walked along the highlighted route, turned out to be a beautifully landscaped and maintained graveyard with dozens of private family mausoleums, many of them large, ornate, and obviously extraordinarily expensive. Several of them looked like small Greek temples, while one mauso-leum I walked by was a pyramid that had the family members buried in the sides. The individuals buried there, I thought as I kept the map of the graveyard oriented to the direction I was walking, must have believed that, like the Egyptian pharaohs, building a large, elaborate burial site would somehow ensure their immortality.

Beckwith's grave, I discovered as I examined the map when I came to a crossroads, sat atop the largest hill in the graveyard. I stood for several seconds looking up the hill, realizing what

I would be seeing in a few moments. How many people have ever had the opportunity to visit the spot where they were buried? How many people have ever had the chance to see their own gravesite? However, a few minutes later, as I neared the top of the hill, I felt my heart thumping against my rib cage and found I was breathing like a nonswimmer who had surfaced after unexpectedly going under water. Even though the air felt pleasantly cool, I also felt little rivulets of sweat running down my sides. I couldn't believe it. This was ridiculous. I knew the climb up the hill hadn't been that strenuous and that I was in much too good condition to have my heart beat so hard and my breath become so ragged. The previous year, my brother Fred and I had hiked to the bottom of the Grand Canyon and back up. To prepare for this trek, which is an eighteen-mile round-trip (eight miles down on one trail and ten miles back up on another), I had trained intensely for a year, which I then continued afterward. My heart, however, hadn't beaten this hard after climbing ten miles to the top of the Grand Canyon. My breathing, even in the thin air at the top of the canyon, hadn't been this painfully rapid.

I stopped at the top of the hill to get myself under control. It didn't take me long to recognize an anxiety attack. When I was a rookie officer, frightening situations, such as going into a dark warehouse looking for burglars or entering a home where I knew someone inside was armed and had already hurt someone, would always bring one on. My heart would start beating in my chest like a drummer on a sugar high, my sweat glands would gush out their liquid stores, and my breathing would become short, ragged gasps. Two other physical symptoms, I found, also usually accompanied these high-anxiety situations: my left knee would shake uncontrollably and my hands would tingle from the cold electricity of adrenalin. As a rookie officer, I had always overcome this by simply ignoring these symptoms, locking my left knee, and charging into the situations, hoping no one knew how really frightened I was.

Fortunately, after spending enough years as a police officer, individuals usually lose this intense fear at such situations because they know what to expect after being involved in enough high-risk incidents. Veteran officers know what the most likely actions of the people they are dealing with will be, and they are prepared to respond to them. Most of the intense anxiety symptoms rookies suffer disappear with time and experience.

However, as I stood at the top of the hill looking at Beckwith's gravesite fifty feet away and realized I didn't know what to expect, I found my left knee quivering and my hands tingling. I felt like a rookie officer again. I stood in the spot for several minutes, taking deep breaths and telling myself that I was being foolish, but the symptoms didn't let up. Intellectually, I realized I had nothing to be frightened of, but I couldn't seem to convince my body. I knew there couldn't be any ghosts or spirits here because the spirit that had been in Beckwith's body was now in mine. But my body wouldn't listen to my brain. My body realized I had never been in this situation before, and that I had no idea what to expect. Finally, I did what I had done dozens of times as a rookie: I took several deep breaths, locked my left knee, and charged into the situation.

When I walked toward the site highlighted on the plot map, my knee continued to shake no matter how much I tried to stop it. Beckwith's grave marker, I discovered as I approached it as cautiously as I would a snarling dog, turned out to be a low stone bench, where I imagined Bertha had come and sat. I stopped several feet away and stood looking at the grave for probably a minute. Nothing out of the ordinary happened, yet still my body kept itself operating at high alert. My heart continued to beat hard and fast, and my breath still came short and ragged. But, along with all of these symptoms, my bladder and bowels also suddenly felt very full, another rookie symptom. How much adrenalin could a body have, I wondered, as the electricity, like waves pounding on a shore, surged out my arms and into my hands.

I tried to think of what could be causing these symptoms because I felt if I knew, then I could devise a strategy to deal with it. Was it because I knew I had died before and was afraid to face it, knowing that it would happen again? Was it because I expected something supernatural to happen at the gravesite? The problem was I just didn't know.

Finally, I said out loud, as if I needed to do that in order to convince myself it was true, "Dammit, Bob, you've been a police officer for thirty years, and you're acting like an eleven-year-old kid on Halloween! Now quit it! There's absolutely nothing to be frightened of!" However, no matter how strenuously I told myself this, I realized I wasn't going to convince my body that nothing was wrong. The anxiety attack continued without any signs of abating. And yet, though I knew clearly what would stop the anxiety (getting out of there), I also knew I couldn't leave without somehow showing myself that I had overcome the fear. Nearby I saw two workmen trimming some hedges, and I immediately knew what I needed to do.

I took a deep breath and walked over and asked one of the workers if he would assist me by taking my picture at the grave, finding that my symptoms had begun to lessen the moment I left the gravesite. This told me that it was the grave itself that was causing the symptoms, but still not why. When we walked back to the grave, however, the symptoms returned full force, and so I planted my left leg, locked my knee, and tried to look calm for the photo. But an eternity passed as I waited for the picture to be taken. The man I had asked to help me seemed to work forever focusing the shot. Finally though, when I heard the click of the camera shutter, I figured I had given enough proof I had overcome the fear. I still didn't know what was causing the anxiety, but felt truly thankful that nothing supernatural had occurred at the grave because I just don't know how I would have dealt with it. I collected the camera, thanked the man for his assistance, and headed out of the graveyard, never to return. Ever.

Chapter Fifteen

January 2015

In the fifteen years since the first publication of this book, a lot has happened because of it. But before I get into that, several things haven't happened. One of the things that hasn't happened is a return to the graveyard, even though I have been asked many times if I had ever gone back. There is no reason, as far as I can see, to put myself under that kind of stress simply to prove I could do it. Would it be easier the second time because of all I know now? I'll never find out.

Another thing that hasn't happened is more regression sessions. A number of people have asked me if I ever returned for another regression session after I finished my investigation. I haven't, and for a very good reason. By the time I finished my investigation I had read over 14,000 pages of Beckwith's diary, his autobiography, many references to him from other sources, and I studied his scrapbooks. So, even if I could access

Beckwith's life during a regression session, I could never be certain that what I saw came from a genuine memory rather than just from something I had read during my investigation.

However, one of the things that has happened is that I have uncovered evidence that answers question #11, Beckwith using the name Jack, and question #16, his wife's name sounding like Amanda. These two questions, I felt, were a partial confirmation and a miss.

The answers to these questions came about because of one of the really fun things about being a writer, and that is receiving correspondence from your readers. Naturally, it is always gratifying to hear about how your writing has been appreciated and how it has even inspired your readers. But also, many times readers will want to point out things that they know or have found out, which they believe should have been included in your book.

After the publication of the first edition of this book in 1999, I heard from dozens of readers who applauded my courage for writing it and who told me about how my experiences had jelled with their own experiences and beliefs. But, along with this, I also heard from three readers who had done considerable research into some of the facts of my book. One of these facts occurred in Chapter 2, where I tell about suddenly blurting out during the regression that my name was Jack, which was #11 on my list of 28 questions. Of course, Jack is a nickname for John, and as it turned out Beckwith's first name was James. One reader did a considerable amount of research, which she sent me copies of, that said that in the middle and late 1800s, Jack was a nickname not just for John, but also for James. And given that Beckwith had always hated the name James, identifying himself as Jack suddenly became a much more likely possibility.

I also heard from a gentleman who worked as a researcher at the John Singer Sargent Catalogue Raisonne in New York City. He had happened upon the first edition of this book, read it, and wrote to me that he thought it was "a riveting story, one which you tell very well—a real page turner." In his letter, he also wanted to offer an explanation for the use of the name Jack in my regression. The researcher pointed out to me that in French the name James is Jacques, and that Beckwith, who spent five years in France, could very well have used that in the place of James. As further evidence of this, Beckwith wrote often in his diary about his love of the French culture, and he many times used French words and expressions in his diary.

Another reader, a New York State librarian who lived and worked close to where the original Beckwith farm had been in Oxford, and where a young Carroll Beckwith had spent many summers, wrote to tell me about finding two portraits stored in the basement of the library. She discovered that these portraits had been painted by Carroll Beckwith. Not recognizing the name, the librarian did some research on him and found my book, which she read. Inspired, she then began doing some local research and discovered that Beckwith had dated a young woman from the area, and that this woman had moved to

New York City at the same time that Beckwith lived there. Her name? Almeda.

Could this be the woman in Chapter 2 that I saw Beckwith meeting on a street in New York City? This also seems a distinct possibility.

Along with hearing from readers, I also heard from a number of media outlets. As might be imagined, a book of this sort written by a veteran police officer attracted quite a bit of media attention, so I ended up appearing on a number of television and radio shows. In January 2000, for example, soon after publication of the first edition, I appeared on *The Art Bell Show*. This is a radio show that regularly discusses New Age concepts and has a huge audience. I appeared on a segment of it hosted by Whitley Strieber, the author of a number of New Age books.

In addition to appearing on over a dozen radio programs, this book also got me on television. Soon after its publication, I received a telephone call from the producers of a television program called *Beyond Chance*. The caller said that the producers would like me to appear on a segment of their show. Naturally, I said yes, and they came with a truckload of cameras and equipment to my home and filmed what I felt turned out to be a very fair report on my experience. Following this, I also filmed segments about this book for *Northwest Afternoon*, the local PBS station, the *National Enquirer Television Show*, and *In Search Of*. In September of 2013 I even appeared on *The Katie Couric Show* in New York City to discuss my investigation of Carroll Beckwith.

However, the television program that caused me the most concern and had the most negative impact was one called *Proof Positive*. Several years after the first publication of this book, and after I had already been on a number of national television programs about it, I received a call at the Homicide Office. The caller identified herself as Sally Kaplan. She told me that she worked for Cosgrove Meurer Productions, which had produced the popular television program *Unsolved Mysteries*. They were now, she said, producing a show called *Proof Positive*. This program would, she told me, subject claims such as the ones I had made in this book to scientific investigation. And so, she added, the producers wanted to know if I would be willing to take a lie detector test on national television.

Of course, I immediately said yes because I had included nothing in this book that wasn't 100 percent true. But then very soon after hanging up, I began to worry about my decision.

I wasn't worried at all about the things I had included in this book, because, as I said, they were all true. But I certainly did worry about trusting my reputation to a device that scientific research has shown to be only 70 to 90 percent accurate, a level of trustworthiness that the courts feel is too low to allow as evidence. I realized with a stomach-knotting dread that this meant, on the average, one out of every five times the operator will say that a person is telling the truth when he or she is actually lying, or, much more worrisome to me, that one out of every five times the operator will claim that the person is lying when he or she is actually telling the truth. Was I setting myself up to be embarrassed on national television?

Naturally, it was too late to change my mind, because that would have really looked suspect. So I knew that the only thing I could do was just go through with it. As it turned out, I actually took two lie detector tests for the show, one in Indianapolis and one in New York City. The part of the segment filmed in New York City, despite the anxiety of taking the lie detector test, had some very beneficial side effects. The show rented out the National Academy of Design for that day, and as part of the filming I got to look at and handle Carroll Beckwith's actual diaries, a very moving moment for me considering that I had spent a year reading microfilm copies of them. And much to my relief, I didn't encounter any of the negative statistical problems I had feared with the lie detector tests.

It was following the airing of this show, however, that I began to experience the negative consequences I had feared when I finally decided that, despite the possible consequences, I needed to go public with my information. A few months before the *Proof Positive* segment aired on national television, a local alternative news magazine called *NUVO* had contacted and interviewed me about this book. As a consequence of the interview, *NUVO* did a feature article about this book and put my picture on their cover with the caption: "Captain Karma." There are dozens of *NUVO* news boxes all over downtown Indianapolis, and for a week my face appeared on them.

When this event occurred, I had been a police officer for more than thirty-five years, and during this time I had trained, mentored, and helped many younger officers who had gone on to be promoted. I had always felt it important to nurture and guide individuals who I thought could be the future leadership of the police department. As a result, over half of the Chief's Command Staff at this time had worked for me in the past, and many of them felt a loyalty to me for my help. Consequently, when this book began getting a lot of media attention, I began receiving feedback from several members of the Chief's Command Staff about the administration's reaction to it, which grew more and more negative with each bit of media attention.

I heard from several of my sources that this *NUVO* article had caused the administration considerable concern, though they didn't decide to take any action on it. Then, a few months later, the segment about Beckwith appeared on *Proof Positive*. Soon after this, the police department abruptly removed me from my position as commander of the Homicide Branch and transferred me to the Citizens Service Desk, the office the public comes to when they want to be fingerprinted or obtain a police report. This is a spot usually reserved for captains just getting ready to retire, which my sources on the Chief's Command Staff told me was the message I was supposed to get.

The interesting part about this move was that six years earlier, when I had been assigned to take over the command of the Homicide Branch, Indianapolis had experienced its bloodiest year ever. My mission, the chief told me, was to bring down the number of homicides. And for the next six years, the number of homicides dropped steadily. When the administration abruptly removed me as commander of the Homicide Branch, the city was experiencing the lowest number of homicides it had seen in almost twenty years, and our clearance rate stood at 83 percent, a number unheard of for a large police department. Apparently, however, my journey into the arena of reincarnation simply didn't fit with what the administration felt a police captain should be doing.

And yet, while through my sources on the Chief's Command Staff I knew the real reason for my sudden transfer, no one, of course, would officially confirm it. That would have treaded dangerously into a violation of the First Amendment. But interestingly enough, soon after my move to the Citizens Service Desk, I sold a movie option on this book and a screenwriter came to Indianapolis to write the screenplay. When I introduced the screenwriter around the police department, he asked one of the senior administrators point blank if I had been moved out of Homicide because of this book. The administrator jumped up from the desk and went into a ten-minute tirade about how that wasn't true, exclaiming a half dozen times, "Put a dozen Bibles right here and I'll swear on them that it's not true!" As anyone experienced in interrogation will confirm, this type of repeated exclamation is usually an indication of falsehood. But despite this, my career at the police department never recovered after my removal from Homicide, and I did decide to retire several years later.

But this wasn't the end of it. As I additionally feared, the publication of this book also negatively affected my writing career. Before this book came out, I had been publishing a book a year about police procedure. It would be six years before I would get my next book contract.

Despite these problems, though, all of the reaction to this book certainly wasn't negative. I talked to many police officers who told me how inspiring they found my book to be and how they had always believed that reincarnation was possible. As I related earlier, police officers as a group have a large number of experiences with the paranormal, and so for many of them, this book didn't seem that unusual.

The reaction of the general public to this book has also been very positive. Although I did have a woman one time on a radio call-in show tell me that I was going to Hell for writing it, many readers have told me how this book has inspired them, even though many of them had questions about subjects they felt I hadn't dealt deeply enough within the book. One of the questions I've heard often is about my wife, and how she could have witnessed all the things she did and still not believe in reincarnation. I have even been asked by groups I was going to speak to bring her along so that they could ask her.

Well, fifteen years since the first publication of this book and my wife still resists believing in reincarnation. My only answer as to why this is so comes from my own experiences. The hardest part for me when I finished the investigation into my past-life regression wasn't accepting the facts I had discovered, but rather accepting that I needed to change my concept of how the world worked. To accept this new view, I had to totally discard my old belief system and be willing to live under an entirely new one. I had to accept that the world was completely different from what I had believed it to be my whole life. I suddenly felt like Beckwith when he was faced with accepting the many radical changes in the art world. Changing a view of the world a person has held for a lifetime is not an easy thing to do. I went through a period of intense personal struggle before I could come to terms with the idea that the worldview I had held for decades was wrong, and that the world apparently operated on parameters I had never imagined. And this, I suspect, can be particularly difficult for individuals who have been thoroughly indoctrinated in the traditional religious view of how the world operates and have accepted this viewpoint all of their lives without question. It is like being asked to erase a program a person has worked with for his or her entire life and replace it with a new program the person is totally unfamiliar with. This is an incredibly difficult thing to do, and I think that some people just simply can't.

Along with questions about my wife, I have also received a large amount of other feedback from readers of this book, feedback that has made me feel even more certain that my decision to go public was the right one. Many readers have written to me wanting to share their own experiences. Some have had déjà vu events at locations they have never been to before, others have had dreams about past lives, some have wanted to share their own evidence of a past life, and some have just wanted to try past-life regression themselves. Many readers contacted me in order to find out how to get in touch with Dr. Griffith to set up their own past-life regression session. Dr. Griffith, however, has since retired and is no longer seeing clients. Cathy Graban, now Cathy Gregory, has also retired and now works as a psychotherapist in Indianapolis.

But without a doubt, my most fulfilling moment since writing this book came when a doctor I appeared with on a television show told me about giving copies of my book to terminally ill patients, with the intent of lessening their fear of dying. If only for this reason alone, the publication of this book has been more than worthwhile. When I think about this, I see how small my own problems at the police department turned out to be, and I know that my decision to go public was the right one.

Conclusion

What Does It All Mean?

Ever since the first publication of this book I've often asked myself the question "What does everything I've found mean?" My pondering of this question, however, highlights certain shortcomings on my part, since I was a cop, not a philosopher or a theologian. I've found this to be a very serious drawback in my search for the answer to this question because the answer seems to have deep philosophical and theological implications. I cannot accept that with the billions of people who have inhabited the Earth, my case is unique, that mine would be the only case since John the Baptist, who Jesus describes in the book of Matthew as being a rebirth of the prophet Elijah.

Even pondering how I came to the successful conclusion of this investigation raises many of the same issues. Believing that I could see a specific painting during my regression, and then just happen to visit the city where this painting resided at that moment, and then just happen to visit the obscure little art gallery where it just happened to be exhibited stretches credibility far beyond the possibility of it all being just one big coincidence.

But in addition, this problem is compounded by the fact that this one incident, as it turned out, wasn't the only time in my investigation when what at the moment appeared to be a startling coincidence dumped information about Carroll Beckwith literally into my lap. There were several. For example, when I was interviewing art dealers in my search for what had happened to the portrait of the hunchbacked woman, one of the dealers handed me a copy of *American Art Review* as an example of how dealers know what paintings other dealers have. I opened the magazine, and the first thing I saw was a picture of a Beckwith painting titled *Greene.* When I later talked to the art dealer who owned *Greene,* he put me in contact with an expert on American painters he used. This expert, though not knowing the location of the hunchbacked woman portrait, did, without my asking, inform me of the whereabouts of the Beckwith scrapbooks, whose location, until that time, I had been unable to determine.

If these two had been the only startling coincidences that had occurred, I probably could have forced myself to write them off as being just startling coincidences. But they weren't. There were many more, which my training as an investigator rather than a philosopher or a theologian told me was wrong, that something was going on beyond mere coincidences. What though, I didn't know.

And yet, despite my lack of training in philosophy and theology, I still feel I am more than qualified to talk about what the findings of this investigation have meant to my life. Before I had my regression with Dr. Griffith and then investigated what I had experienced, I suppose I could have been called a non-involved Christian. I had been raised by a very religious mother and had attended church regularly as a child. But regardless, I had a lot of questions about life that the lessons I had learned in church just didn't seem to answer, particularly questions about the unfairness of life. I wondered, for example, why, if we only have one life, God would inflict some people with childhood diseases, physical deformities, abject poverty, physical cruelties, and many other unpleasant things, while at the same time allowing other people to live lives of ease, with few major problems. This question grew even more important when, as a police officer, and particularly while working in Homicide, I saw hundreds of people, many of them barely starting out in their life, lose their lives violently and often senselessly. It all seemed so unfair, and no one in all of my years of attending church ever discussed or answered the question of why God would allow this.

I finally received an answer to this question when, following the first publication of this book, I talked to hundreds of people about past lives and about their own past-life regressions. Everyone, I discovered, experiences many lives, and in each of these lives they have specific goals to reach. But more important, individuals would tell me that some of their lives had been good, some not so good, and some terrible. I discovered through this that there exists a real fairness in life after all because everyone gets a chance at all of the different lives. A wealthy person living a life of ease could well have been an outcast living in poverty in the preceding life. It all evens out. Life suddenly made sense to me.

During these intervening years, I have also discovered an important side benefit to my investigation of Carroll Beckwith: it has broadened my outlook on life. As a police officer, I often saw things in terms of right or wrong, no in between. If something couldn't be seen and felt, it wasn't true. However, since I have proven reincarnation to be true, I now find myself not rejecting things just because they don't sound rock solid and absolutely provable. While I certainly don't wholeheartedly accept every philosophy or belief system I encounter, I don't immediately reject them out of hand either.

In addition to this, before my investigation into Beckwith, my life as Bob Snow seemed to be simply a string of events that had no pattern or connection. But after the investigation, I discovered that I was looking at my life through the wrong viewpoint. When I began looking at life through the philosophy of reincarnation and how in each of many lives a person has certain set goals to accomplish, I could see that everything Beckwith experienced in his life and everything I have experienced in this life, from wanting (since a child of four or five) to be a writer, to being an overachiever, to becoming a police investigator, were all pointing me toward one goal. They all made the writing of this book possible. And so, everything that happened, even those incidents that came at a high cost, were well worth it. It was all part of reaching my goal.

The End

GET MORE AT LLEWELLYN.COM

Visit us online to browse hundreds of our books and decks, plus sign up to receive our e-newsletters and exclusive online offers.

- **Free tarot readings** • **Spell-a-Day** • **Moon phases**
- **Recipes, spells, and tips** • **Blogs** • **Encyclopedia**
- **Author interviews, articles, and upcoming events**

GET SOCIAL WITH LLEWELLYN

Find us on Facebook

www.Facebook.com/LlewellynBooks

Follow us on twitter™

www.Twitter.com/Llewellynbooks

GET BOOKS AT LLEWELLYN

JUDITH
MARSHALL

PAST LIVES
PRESENT
STORIES

Healing & Wisdom Through
Past Life Exploration

Past Lives, Present Stories
Healing & Wisdom Through Past Life Exploration
JUDITH MARSHALL

Discover how flashes from past lives can appear as signs and synchronicities, childhood impressions, dreams and memories, even spontaneous shifts in consciousness or time. Providing time-tested exercises, *Past Lives, Present Stories* shows how to explore your past lives and use the lessons you've learned to flourish in your present incarnation.

Join author Judith Marshall as she takes you through the full range of techniques for exploring your past lives and piecing together information to help you on your path. Providing examples of her own glimpses into her past lives, Judith illustrates how illuminating and healing past-life discovery can be.

978-0-7387-3668-6, 240 pp., 5³⁄₁₆ x 8   **$15.99**

To order, call 1-877-NEW-WRLD
Prices subject to change without notice
Order at Llewellyn.com 24 hours a day, 7 days a week

One Woman's Exploration
of Her Past Lives

REINCARNATION

MARILOU TRASK-CURTIN

Reincarnation

One Woman's Exploration of Her Past Lives
Marilou Trask-Curtin

As a three-month-old baby lying in her grandmother's arms, author Marilou Trask-Curtin had the fantastic experience of remembering herself in other bodies, times, and places. In this fascinating book, she tells the stories of soul lessons and past-life relationships that were too powerful to ignore. With a supportive community of like-minded seekers, Trask-Curtin achieves a remarkable transformation, and now she is able to affirm this important fact: Reincarnation is real.

It's not easy for anyone to move past the limiting teachings of our culture, but *Reincarnation* shares a comforting idea— death is not the end, but rather a glorious new beginning. Join Marilou as she explores her soul's path, returning again and again to fulfill what was unfulfilled in other lifetimes. With the true stories of Marilou's remarkable experiences, this book reaffirms that empathy, forgiveness, and unconditional love are our soul's most important lessons.

978-0-7387-3897-0, 240 pp., 5³⁄₁₆ x 8   **$14.99**